How To Use This Study Guide

This 20-lesson study guide corresponds to *"WEAPONS!" With Rick Renner* (**Renner TV**). Each lesson in this study guide covers a topic that is addressed during the program series, with questions and references supplied to draw you deeper into your own private study of the Scriptures on this subject.

To derive the most benefit from this study guide, consider the following:

First, watch or listen to the program prior to working through the corresponding lesson in this guide. (Programs can also be viewed at **renner.org** by clicking on the Media/Archives links or on our Renner Ministries YouTube channel.)

Second, take the time to look up the scriptures included in each lesson. Prayerfully consider their application to your own life.

Third, use a journal or notebook to make note of your answers to each lesson's Study Questions and Practical Application challenges.

Fourth, invest specific time in prayer and in the Word of God to consult with the Holy Spirit. Write down the scriptures or insights He reveals to you.

Finally, take action! Whatever the Lord tells you to do according to His Word, do it.

For added insights on this subject, it is recommended that you obtain Rick Renner's books *Dressed to Kill: A Biblical Approach to Spiritual Warfare and Armor* and *Spiritual Weapons To Defeat the Enemy: Overcoming the Wiles, Devices, and Deception of the Devil.* You may also select from Rick's other available resources by placing your order at **renner.org** or by calling 1-800-742-5593.

TOPIC

THIS IS WAR!

SCRIPTURES

1. **Exodus 15:3** — The Lord is a man of war: the Lord is his name.

2. **Exodus 15:4-6** — Pharaoh's chariots and his host hath he cast into the sea: his chosen captains also are drowned in the Red sea. The depths have covered them: they sank into the bottom as a stone. Thy right hand, O Lord, is become glorious in power: thy right hand, O Lord, hath dashed in pieces the enemy.

3. **Exodus 15:7-9** — And in the greatness of thine excellency thou hast overthrown them that rose up against thee: thou sentest forth thy wrath, which consumed them as stubble. And with the blast of thy nostrils the waters were gathered together, the floods stood upright as an heap, and the depths were congealed in the heart of the sea. The enemy said, I will pursue, I will overtake, I will divide the spoil; my lust shall be satisfied upon them; I will draw my sword, my hand shall destroy them.

4. **Exodus 15:10-12** — Thou didst blow with thy wind, the sea covered them: they sank as lead in the mighty waters. Who is like unto thee, O Lord, among the gods? who is like thee, glorious in holiness, fearful in praises, doing wonders? Thou stretchedst out thy right hand, the earth swallowed them.

5. **Psalm 2:1-4** — Why do the heathen rage, and the people imagine a vain thing? The kings of the earth set themselves, and the rulers take counsel together, against the Lord, and against his anointed, saying, Let us break their bands asunder, and cast away their cords from us. He that sitteth in the heavens shall laugh: the Lord shall have them in derision.

6. **Psalm 24:8** — Who is this King of glory? The Lord strong and mighty, the Lord mighty in battle.

7. **1 Samuel 17:45** — Then said David to the Philistine, Thou comest to me with a sword, and with a spear, and with a shield: but I come to

A Note From Rick Renner

I am on a personal quest to see a "revival of the Bible" so people can establish their lives on a firm foundation that will stand strong and endure the test as end-time storm winds begin to intensify.

In order to experience a revival of the Bible in your personal life, it is important to take time each day to read, receive, and apply its truths to your life. James tells us that if we will continue in the perfect law of liberty — refusing to be forgetful hearers, but determined to be doers — we will be blessed in our ways. As you watch or listen to the programs in this series and work through this corresponding study guide, I trust you will search the Scriptures and allow the Holy Spirit to help you hear something new from God's Word that applies specifically to your life. I encourage you to be a doer of the Word He reveals to you. Whatever the cost, I assure you — it will be worth it.

> Thy words were found, and I did eat them;
> and thy word was unto me the joy and rejoicing of mine heart:
> for I am called by thy name, O Lord God of hosts.
> — Jeremiah 15:16

Your brother and friend in Jesus Christ,

Rick Renner

Rick Renner

WEAPONS!
Everything the New Testament Says About Spiritual Weapons in One Series

Copyright © 2024 by Rick Renner
1814 W. Tacoma St.
Broken Arrow, OK 74012-1406

Published by Rick Renner Ministries
www.renner.org

ISBN 13: 978-1-6675-1128-3

ISBN 13 eBook: 978-1-6675-1129-0

thee in the name of the Lord of hosts, the God of the armies of Israel, whom thou hast defied.

8. **Isaiah 42:13** — The Lord shall go forth as a mighty man, he shall stir up jealousy like a man of war: he shall cry, yea, roar; he shall prevail against his enemies.

9. **Luke 2:13** — And suddenly there was with the angel a multitude of the heavenly host…

10. **1 John 3:8** — …For this purpose the Son of God was manifested, that he might destroy the works of the devil.

11. **John 1:27** — He it is, who coming after me is preferred before me, whose shoe's latchet I am not worthy to unloose.

GREEK WORDS

1. "destroy" — λύω (luo): to loosen; to set free; to untie; to unravel

2. "Lord" — Κύριος (Kurios): Lord; Supreme Master; One with complete authority over every known, unknown, visible, or invisible realm

SYNOPSIS

WEAPONS! is a powerful teaching that focuses on the spiritual weaponry made available to us through the death, burial, and resurrection of Jesus Christ. The 20 lessons in this study guide will focus on the following topics:

- THIS IS WAR!
- Batten Down the Hatches
- Power for the Fight
- How To Put on the Whole Armor of God
- Five Words of Warfare
- Unseen Spiritual Forces
- What the Bible Teaches About Demons
- An Example of Spiritual Warfare
- The Whole Armor of God
- The Most Important Piece of Weaponry — the Loinbelt of Truth
- The Breastplate of Righteousness

- The Shoes of Peace
- The Shield of Faith
- The Helmet of Salvation
- The Sword of the Spirit
- The Lance of Intercession
- The Flesh Counts for Nothing
- Weapons Are Mighty Through God
- How To Cast Down Imaginations
- Eliminating the Giants in Your Life

The emphasis of this lesson:

We are living in the last of the last days when Satan's evil influence and threats can be seen, heard, and felt all around us. But we serve the God who sits in the heavens and laughs at the plans of the enemy — for, in the end, only His plans will prevail. God is a Man of War; His right hand dashes the enemy to pieces. He is the King of Glory and is strong and mighty in battle. He is the Lord of Heaven's armies!

A PROPHETIC WORD FROM THE LORD

Each year in the late summer and fall months, Rick Renner prepares his heart to hear from the Lord regarding the upcoming year and whatever the Lord might want to say to Rick and his family and to his friends and partners of RENNER Ministries. Here is what the Lord told Rick about the year 2025:

A Storm Is Coming — Spiritual War!
Batten Down the Hatches!

We're headed into a season of intense warfare on many fronts — *economical*, *political*, and *spiritual*. But the Lord is a Man of War, and He knows exactly how to strategize against and overcome every assault against His people and against His Truth.

But just as one should batten down the hatches in a time of storms, God's people must be mentally and spiritually prepared for a stormy season that lies directly ahead. But with the grace of

God, the power of the Holy Spirit, the promises of God's Word, and the weaponry He has given, we can move forward step by step with the strategic guidance of the Holy Spirit. And God will triumphantly lead His people forward and will carry out His plans for this end-time age.

This is not a time to fear, moan, or cry, but a time to *rejoice*, for God is strategically at work even in ways that you do not see. Although it may seem the enemy and those he is influencing are derailing God's purposes, remember that the One who sits in the heavens laughs at their plans, and He will ultimately have them in derision (*see* Psalm 2:4). God is a Man of War, and in the end, His purposes shall surely prevail.

What a powerful word for 2025! Within this important word from the Lord are two poignant pictures: the image of warfare and the image of a storm. It is vital we keep both in mind as we progress into 2025 and prepare for the coming storms. But we don't have to face the coming challenges alone!

The Lord is a Man of War, and there is no better warrior than God Himself. He knows how to overcome every attack of the enemy, and He has given us several key spiritual weapons so we can be victorious!

'The Lord Is a Man of War' — the Oldest Song in the Bible

The phrase "The Lord is a Man of War" comes from Exodus, after Pharaoh and his armies had just been defeated and had sunk to the bottom of the Red Sea. In Exodus 15:3, Moses and the children of Israel sang, "The Lord is a man of war: The Lord is his name." This is actually the oldest recorded song in the Bible!

The term "a man of war" describes *an imminent warrior — one who is mighty in battle or who understands how to fight and vanquish his foes.* And that is who our God is!

The song continues in Exodus 15:4-6:

> **Pharaoh's chariots and his host hath he cast into the sea: His chosen captains also are drowned in the Red sea. The depths have covered them: They sank into the bottom as a stone. Thy**

right hand, O Lord, is become glorious in power: Thy right hand, O Lord, hath dashed in pieces the enemy.

We serve a powerful and mighty God. It doesn't matter what is going on in the world around us because God is in charge, and He knows how to fight. He knows how to undo every assault of the enemy. Jesus really is Lord, and He is a Man of War!

The next part of this song Moses and the children of Israel sang goes into what we might hear from our enemies.

And in the greatness of thine excellency thou hast overthrown them that rose up against thee: Thou sentest forth thy wrath, which consumed them as stubble. And with the blast of thy nostrils the waters were gathered together, the floods stood upright as an heap, and the depths were congealed in the heart of the sea. The enemy said, I will pursue, I will overtake, I will divide the spoil; my lust shall be satisfied upon them; I will draw my sword, my hand shall destroy them.

— Exodus 15:47-9

Even today, our enemies continue to say the very same thing they said in the days of Moses. They want you to believe they are winning by saying, "We've got the upper hand. We're going to destroy the cause of God. We will take all power into our hands and will satisfy ourselves." But in Exodus 15:10-12, we find how God responded to Pharaoh and his forces when they had said those things:

Thou didst blow with thy wind, the sea covered them: They sank as lead in the mighty waters. Who is like unto thee, O Lord, among the gods? Who is like thee, glorious in holiness, fearful in praises, doing wonders? Thou stretchedst out thy right hand, the earth swallowed them.

God understands how to fight and how to vanquish every foe that comes against Him, His people, or His cause. We don't need to fear the boasts of the enemy because Jesus truly is Lord. He is in charge, and He will have His way in spite of what evil forces try to do to thwart His plan.

God Sits in Heaven and Laughs

Have you ever looked around at society and felt like the culture surrounding you is raging against the truths of God's Word? Has it ever seemed like there is a battle for control over the airwaves, media, and every other facet of life? While the enemy and his cohorts may think they're succeeding or that they're in control, they're not. God is in control, and nothing can thwart His plans.

A great example of this, as well as an accurate depiction of the time we are living in now, can be found in Psalm 2.

> **Why do the heathen rage, and the people imagine a vain thing? The kings of the earth set themselves, and the rulers take counsel together, against the Lord, and against his anointed, saying, Let us break their bands asunder, and cast away their cords from us.**
>
> **— Psalm 2:1-3**

This is what is happening today behind closed doors and in private places. There are people devising plans against the Lord and plotting to take charge. Man has his own plan, but Psalm 2:4 gloriously declares, "He that sitteth in the heavens shall laugh: the Lord shall have them in derision."

While politicians are making their plans and people with great wealth are scheming up all kinds of conspiracies to control society surrounding us, the Lord is watching it all. While people are sitting around their tables conspiring, God is looking in and laughing. He scoffs at them and their plans. These schemers believe they are in charge when, in fact, God is working His plan and they are completely unaware of it.

Psalm 24:8 says, "Who is this King of glory? The Lord strong and mighty, the Lord mighty in battle." The King of Glory referred to here is Jesus, and He is the One we serve. Just as we saw in Exodus 15:3, once again we see that God is a Man of War, and He is strong and mighty in battle!

Facing Insurmountable Opposition

In First Samuel 17, we find the well-known story of David facing Goliath. When looking at only the natural side of things, Goliath probably looked insurmountable. He was a massive giant — a Nephilim — while David was a mere youth. In the natural, David was no match for Goliath. Yet when confronted with Goliath's threats, David responded with boldness.

First Samuel 17:45 says, "Then said David to the Philistine, Thou comest to me with a sword, and with a spear, and with a shield: but I come to thee in the name of the Lord of hosts, the God of the armies of Israel, whom thou hast defied."

David demonstrated exactly how we should respond each time the enemy tries to derail the purposes of God in our lives. Goliath defied God, and it was a serious matter to do so.

In fact, we have multiple examples of God swinging into action to deal with those who defied Him. For example, when we look again at the story of Moses (*see* Exodus 7-11), Pharaoh repeatedly defied the name of the Lord and challenged the superiority of the true God. In response, God demonstrated just who He really was! One by one, God discounted every god the Egyptians worshiped until even Pharaoh himself finally acknowledged that God was indeed God and Pharaoh's armies were defeated at the Red Sea after they'd continued to defiantly pursue the children of Israel (*see* Exodus 14).

God does not take defiance lightly, and neither should we. As when David stood before Goliath who was defying the living God, we must respond to such defiance the way David did. David shouted, "You come to me with a sword, and with a spear, and with a shield. You come to me with your plans and think you're going to undo me. But I come to you in the name of the Lord of hosts!"

The Lord of the Armies of Heaven

The word "hosts" describes armies. When Jesus is called the "Lord of hosts," it means He is the Lord of the armies of Heaven, and He is the captain over them all.

David said to Goliath, "…I come to thee in the name of the Lord of hosts, the God of the armies of Israel, whom thou hast defied" (1 Samuel 17:45). When the enemy steps across the line in an attempt to defy the Church or defy the plans and purposes of God, he has crossed a line he should not have crossed!

As previously quoted in Psalm 2:4, God sits in the heavens and laughs at the schemes of the enemy, because the Lord is working His own plan, and the enemy is completely unaware of that plan! God simply steps forward with all His heavenly hosts and derails every enemy that defies Him!

'The Lord Shall Go Forth as a Mighty Man — Like a Man of War'

Isaiah 42:13 says, "The Lord shall go forth as a mighty man, he shall stir up jealously like a man of war: he shall cry, yea, roar; he shall prevail against his enemies."

In every situation in which the enemy rises up to defy Him, God will prevail. He will prevail politically. He will prevail economically. He will prevail spiritually. God is a Man of War! He is an imminent warrior and mighty in battle, and He understands how to fight and vanquish every foe!

Some might argue, "But these are all Old Testament examples!" However, there are plenty of examples in the New Testament as well.

In Luke chapter 2, we read that there were a group of shepherds out in a field watching over their flocks at night. Suddenly, the angel of the Lord appeared to them and gave them a message. Verse 13 says, "And suddenly there was with the angel a multitude of the heavenly host...."

Suddenly, all of the armies of Heaven showed up! Why? Because the Creator had been born in Bethlehem. Though He was born as a Babe, He was the Commander-in-Chief who had come to the earth on assignment. He was the Captain and General of all of the heavenly forces, and every angel of Heaven had appeared at His birth to salute Him on His assignment. They acknowledged and recognized who He was. They recognized His authority and every one of the heavenly host came to celebrate their great Commander who had just arrived on the planet Earth on divine assignment!

Unraveled: Totally Destroying the Works of Devil

In First John 3:8, we are told, "...For this purpose the Son of God was manifested, that he might destroy the works of the devil." The word "destroy" is very important because it is a form of the Greek word *luo*, which means *to loosen, to set free, to untie,* or *to unravel.*

An example of this Greek word is found in John 1:27 when John the Baptist said that he was not worthy to untie Jesus' shoes. That word "unloose" or "untie" is *luo.* When shoes are untied, they are unraveled and when they are unraveled, they become loosened. Eventually they become so loose, they no longer have their holding power and begin to fall off the feet!

So when the Bible says, "For this reason the Son of God was manifest, that he might destroy the works of the enemy," the word *luo*, or "destroy," could also be interpreted as, "For this purpose the Son of God was manifested, that he might *untie, unravel, loosen,* and *totally destroy* the works of the enemy."

Jesus totally destroyed principalities and powers with His death, burial, and resurrection. Though the enemy may believe his plan will work against God's plan, and though he may allege that he will derail the purposes of God, the reality is we serve a Man of War! "The Lord is a man of war: The Lord is his name" (Exodus 15:3).

If you feel like the world around you has become a dark place, your observations are correct — it *has*. In fact, the Bible says it will become much darker between now and the Second Coming of Jesus. But the Lord is not disturbed. He is an imminent warrior, mighty in battle; He knows how to attack and vanquish every foe. He is the Lord of hosts! It does not matter what you may be facing in your personal life — He is the victorious warrior you serve, and His name is Jesus!

Rather than moan and cry, we need to rejoice because Jesus will derail the enemy and will have His way in your life and in this age — despite what the devil is trying to do in the economic, political, and spiritual spheres. Jesus truly is Lord of all! The word "Lord" in Greek describes one who has ultimate authority in every realm — seen, unseen, visible, and invisible. That is the Jesus we serve: mighty in battle and Lord of all!

STUDY QUESTIONS

Study to shew thyself approved unto God, a workman that needeth not to be ashamed, rightly dividing the word of truth.
— 2 Timothy 2:15

1. How can we be assured and even rejoice that through God, we will be victorious in this end-time age in which we are living? List at least three strategic resources we have been given.

2. In your own words, explain Psalm 2:1-4. Do you think this verse accurately depicts our current age? What are your thoughts on verse 4?

3. What was the key to David's victory against Goliath? How can we use this same tool in response to times when the enemy tries to derail the purposes of God in our own lives?

4. What is the meaning of the Greek word *luo*? How does this word relate to John the Baptist and the defeat of our enemies?

PRACTICAL APPLICATION

**But be ye doers of the word, and not hearers only,
deceiving your own selves.
— James 1:22**

1. Think of a time in the past when the enemy bombarded you with threatening lies in an attempt to overtake and destroy you. What did you do to overcome those attacks? List verses from God's Word you used as weapons to speak against against and combat those attacks.

2. Reflect on an instance in your life since you were born again when God proved Himself "mighty in battle." Write briefly about your experience.

3. Have you ever faced what seemed to be an impossible circumstance in your life? How did God help you gain the victory?

LESSON 2

TOPIC

Batten Down the Hatches

SCRIPTURES

1. **1 Thessalonians 5:5,6** — Ye are all the children of light, and the children of the day: we are not of the night, nor of darkness. Therefore let us not sleep, as do others; but let us watch and be sober.

2. **1 Thessalonians 5:8** — But let us, who are of the day, be sober, putting on the breastplate of faith and love; and for an helmet, the hope of salvation.

3. **Ephesians 6:14** — Stand therefore, having your loins girt about with truth, and having on the breastplate of righteousness.

4. **Ephesians 6:17** — And take the helmet of salvation...

5. **Ephesians 6:10** — Finally, my brethren, be strong in the Lord, and in the power of his might.

6. **Ephesians 1:5** — Having predestinated us unto the adoption of children by Jesus Christ to himself, according to the good pleasure of his will.

7. **Ephesians 1:7** — In whom we have redemption through his blood, the forgiveness of sins, according to the riches of his grace.

8. **Ephesians 1:11-13** — In whom also we have obtained an inheritance, being predestinated according to the purpose of him who worketh all things after the counsel of his own will: That we should be to the praise of his glory, who first trusted in Christ. In whom ye also trusted, after that ye heard the word of truth, the gospel of your salvation: in whom also after that ye believed, ye were sealed with that holy Spirit of promise.

9. **Ephesians 2:5** — Even when we were dead in sins, hath quickened us together with Christ, (by grace ye are saved).

10. **Ephesians 2:8** — For by grace are ye saved through faith; and that not of yourselves: it is the gift of God.

11. **Ephesians 2:10** — For we are his workmanship, created in Christ Jesus unto good works, which God hath before ordained that we should walk in them.

12. **Ephesians 2:20-22** — And are built upon the foundation of the apostles and prophets, Jesus Christ himself being the chief corner stone; In whom all the building fitly framed together groweth unto an holy temple in the Lord: In whom ye also are builded together for an habitation of God through the Spirit.

13. **Ephesians 3:9-11** — And to make all men see what is the fellowship of the mystery, which from the beginning of the world hath been hid in God, who created all things by Jesus Christ: To the intent that now unto the principalities and powers in heavenly places might be known by the church the manifold wisdom of God, according to the eternal purpose which he purposed in Christ Jesus our Lord.

14. **Ephesians 4:11,12** — And he gave some, apostles; and some, prophets; and some, evangelists; and some, pastors and teachers; for the perfecting of the saints, for the work of the ministry, for the edifying of the body of Christ.

15. **Ephesians 5:1-4** — Be ye therefore followers of God, as dear children; and walk in love, as Christ also hath loved us, and hath given himself for us an offering and a sacrifice to covetousness, let it not be once named among you, as becometh saints; neither filthiness, nor foolish talking, nor jesting, which are not convenient: but rather giving of thanks.

16. **Ephesians 6:1-4** — Children, obey your parents in the Lord: for this is right. Honour thy father and mother; which is the first commandment with promise; that it may be well with thee, and thou mayest live long on the earth. And, ye fathers, provoke not your children to wrath: but bring them up in the nurture and admonition of the Lord.

17. **Ephesians 4:25** — Wherefore putting away lying, speak every man truth with his neighbour: for we are members one of another.

18. **Ephesians 4:27-32** — Neither give place to the devil. Let him that stole steal no more: but rather let him labour, working with his hands the thing which is good, that he may have to give to him that needeth. Let no corrupt communication proceed out of your mouth, but that which is good to the use of edifying, that it may minister grace unto the hearers. And grieve not the holy Spirit of God, whereby ye are sealed unto the day of redemption. Let all bitterness, and wrath, and anger, and clamour, and evil speaking, be put away from you, with all malice: And be ye kind one to another, tenderhearted, forgiving one another, even as God for Christ's sake hath forgiven you.

GREEK WORDS

1. "watch" — γρηγορέω (*gregoreo*): to be on guard; to be attentive; to be awake, as opposed to being sleepy and negligent; to be watchful, as opposed to careless and non-attentive; to give strict attention to; to be cautious; denotes the watchful attitude of one who is on the lookout to make certain no enemy or aggressor successfully gains entry into his life or place of residence; to be on high alert; depicts a person whose attitude is to never let up; to be watchful and wide awake to make certain a sinister force doesn't sneak up to attack and overtake

2. "sober" — νήφω (*nepho*): to keep one's head on straight; to think straight, not like a silly drunk; to be reasonable; describes someone who is sound in the way he lives and thinks; to be sensible; to be serious-minded; to be sober, not drunk; to be sober-minded; to be free from the deliriums, delusions, and hallucinations that may accompany drunkenness; to be

free of silly thinking and, hence, able to have presence of mind and clear judgment, enabling one to be in control of his thinking rather than be controlled by urges, impulses, whims, and fluctuating emotions; to have one's wits about him; to be rational, the opposite of irrational; to be free from a drunken state in which one drops his guard and is more likely to give way to foolish behavior, unreasonable conversations, and detrimental decisions

3. "Finally" — **Τοῦ λοιποῦ** (*Tou loipou*): to the last and most important matter at hand; for the rest of the matter; finally

4. "brother" or "sister" — **ἀδελφός** (*adelphos*) or **ἀδελφὴ** (*adelphe*): a term used to describe two or more who were born from the same womb; an endearing term used to describe those of one's own family; later used in a military sense to depict brothers in battle; a comrade; hence, brotherhood

A PROPHETIC WORD FROM THE LORD

A Storm Is Coming — Spiritual War!
Batten Down the Hatches!

We're headed into a season of intense warfare on many fronts — *economical*, *political*, and *spiritual*. But the Lord is a Man of War, and He knows exactly how to strategize against and overcome every assault against His people and against His Truth.

But just as one should batten down the hatches in a time of storms, God's people must be mentally and spiritually prepared for a stormy season that lies directly ahead. But with the grace of God, the power of the Holy Spirit, the promises of God's Word, and the weaponry He has given, we can move forward step by step with the strategic guidance of the Holy Spirit. And God will triumphantly lead His people forward and will carry out His plans for this end-time age.

This is not a time to fear, moan, or cry, but a time to *rejoice*, for God is strategically at work even in ways that you do not see. Although it may seem the enemy and those he is influencing are derailing God's purposes, remember that the One who sits in the heavens laughs at their plans, and He will ultimately have them in derision (*see* Psalm 2:4). God is a Man of War, and in the end, His purposes shall surely prevail.

SYNOPSIS

We are children of light who have been given spiritual weapons and are exhorted to "watch and be sober." We are not to be stagnant in our walk of faith but, like Paul, are to grow in our understanding of the Word of God. And it is important that we remind ourselves we are not participants in darkness. When we are being attacked, personally and spiritually, like the church of Ephesus, we must stand strong in the Lord — and this is not a suggestion; it is a command. Together, we should stand as brothers and sisters in Christ, fighting as comrades in the trenches of life and proud to be affiliated with one another for we are related by the blood of Jesus. When we remain strong in the Lord, God will gloriously fill us with all the strength we will need to win any battle we are facing in life today.

The emphasis of this lesson:

It is important to be prepared for the battles formed against us by the enemy, Satan. In Chapter 6 of the book of Ephesians, Paul said, "Finally," indicating the tremendous importance of his final thoughts. Due to the struggles the church of Ephesus was facing, he addressed the significance of staying strong in the Lord and using our spiritual weaponry. By referring to the church of Ephesus as his brothers, Paul emphasized the importance of encouraging our brothers and sisters in Christ who have been fighting and struggling — but are still standing — against the onslaught of the attacks of the devil.

Being Sober Children of Light

Have you ever felt like you were surrounded by darkness? Even if you have, the good news is you are not a part of it. You are not a participant in darkness. The Apostle Paul wrote in First Thessalonians 5:5, "Ye are all the children of light, and the children of the day: we are not of the night, nor of darkness."

This verse clearly states that we are children of light and of the day; this is who we are. When we walk in the light, we see what we need to see and know what we need to do. However, since we are children of light, we must be alert. Verse 6 continues:

> **Therefore let us not sleep, as do others; but let us watch and be sober.**
>
> — **1 Thessalonians 5:6**

The word "watch" is from a form of the Greek word *gregoreo*, which means *to be on guard*. It is basically saying, "Let's be on our guard and be sober." The word "sober" is from a form of the Greek word *nepho*, which means *to keep your head on straight*. It's essentially saying, "Don't be like a silly drunk. Be reasonable. Be sound about the way you live and the way you think."

This same Greek word *nepho* — the word for "sober" — is seen once again in verse 8, "But let us, who are of the day, be sober, putting on the breastplate of faith and love; and for an helmet, the hope of salvation." In this instance, the word "sober" means *to be reasonable in the way you live and think*; *to be straight-minded, not like a silly drunk*; or *to be serious-minded*. Notice how Paul began First Thessalonians 5:8, "But let us, who are of the day...." Paul was referring to you and me. He was telling *us* to be reasonable, serious-minded. We need to wake up and be spiritually alert, putting on the breastplate of faith and love.

The Breastplate of Faith and the Helmet of Hope

Paul then instructed believers, "...Putting on the breastplate of faith and love; and for an helmet, the hope of salvation." In this verse, Paul referred to the "breastplate of faith and love," but in Ephesians 6, he called it the "breastplate of righteousness." And in First Thessalonians 5:8, Paul said, "...and for an helmet, the hope of salvation," while in Ephesians 6 he called it simply "...the helmet of salvation."

Why did Paul change the descriptions in these two passages? Well, most scholars agree that the first epistle Paul ever wrote was First Thessalonians. And as Paul was writing First Thessalonians, he began to see and understand, by divine revelation, the spiritual weaponry available to us.

Paul was often confined in a prison for the sake of the Gospel, and there were times he was even chained to a Roman guard. In those situations, Paul had the opportunity to observe the armor of the Roman guards. As Paul sat chained to that Roman guard, the Holy Spirit began to speak to him, "You have spiritual weapons just like they do. You also have a breastplate, helmet, belt, greaves, shoes, shield, sword, and lance." (*See* Ephesians 6:14-18.)

But in First Thessalonians, Paul's understanding of spiritual weaponry was just beginning to develop. When he wrote the epistle of Ephesians years later, Paul's revelation and understanding of spiritual weaponry had developed and increased. In First Thessalonians, his revelation on spiritual weapons had started as a small, primitive list, and then, over the years, his list grew and grew. By the time he wrote Ephesians 6, his list on our spiritual weapons had become quite extensive and profound.

Isn't this encouraging? The longer we walk with the Lord, the greater our revelation can be.

You are supposed to grow in your understanding of the Word of God. You are not supposed to be stagnant. The Holy Spirit will start you in one place, and then He'll expand and expand you. It is important to check in with yourself and ask, *Am I growing in my understanding of the Word of God?*

To the Last And Most Important Point

Turning to Ephesians 6, we come to Paul's expanded list of our spiritual weapons. In Ephesians 6:10, Paul exhorted us, "Finally, my brethren, be strong in the Lord, and in the power of his might." Paul was not misspeaking when he began with the word "Finally." This word in the Greek means *now to the last and most important point.* It seems that Paul saved the most important aspect of what he wanted to say to the very end of his epistle to the Ephesus church: 1) spiritual warfare, and 2) the spiritual weaponry God has made available to us.

This is quite an amazing declaration since Paul discussed so many vitally important truths throughout the book of Ephesians.

Ephesians in Review

In Ephesians 1, Paul wrote about the fact that we were chosen in God before the foundation of the world. That is very important! In Ephesians 1:5, Paul said we have been predestined. In verse 7, he said we have been redeemed. In verses 11 through 13 Paul wrote that we have been sealed with the Holy Spirit. These are all very important truths!

In Ephesians 2, Paul talked about the fact that we have been saved by grace. In verse 10, he wrote about the fact that we have been marvelously created in Christ Jesus. In verses 20 through 22 of the same chapter, we discover that we are the temple of the Holy Spirit and the same Holy Spirit dwells among us all. Each of these revelations is so important to know!

In chapter 3 of Ephesians, Paul described the eternal purpose of God in the Church, and in chapter 4 he described events linked to the fivefold ministry. In chapter 5, Paul told us what to put away, what to put on, and then described the relationships we need to develop with our family and fellow employees.

When we get to Chapter 6, Paul wrote about the relationship between parents and children. He covered so many very important topics in the book of Ephesians.

But when we come to Ephesians 6:10, Paul said, "Finally...." As previously stated, the Greek word for "finally" is *toloipon*, and it means *for the rest of the matter* or *to the last and most important matter at hand*. It is almost as if Paul was saying, "Hey, I've covered a lot of important things, but if you can't remember all of them, I've saved this point to the very end because it is the most important! Finally, to the last and most important matter at hand..." Then Paul began to describe spiritual warfare along with the spiritual weaponry available to us.

But why was this so important for the Ephesians at this particular moment?

Grieving the Holy Spirit

The answer can be found back in Ephesians 4:25-29. Verse 25 reveals the Ephesian believers were lying to each other. The behavior of some believers in Ephesus was so atrocious, verse 27 says they were giving place to the devil. Some were stealing (*see* v. 28), and many were allowing corrupt communication to proceed out of their mouth (v. 29). By the time you come to verse 30, their behavior was so bad, they were beginning to grieve the Holy Spirit!

Then verses 31 and 32 state, "Let all bitterness, and wrath, and anger, and clamour, and evil speaking, be put away from you, with all malice: And be ye kind one to another, tenderhearted, forgiving one another, even as God for Christ's sake hath forgiven you."

The Ephesian church had been reputed to be the most mature and educated church of all of the early churches. The Ephesians had so much head knowledge, but in the practical areas of life, they were failing in many ways. They were struggling in their relationships. They were dealing with wrong attitudes. They were stealing and lying. As stated, their behavior was so terrible, Ephesians 4:30 records they were grieving the Holy Spirit. Even though the believers in Ephesus had minds filled with information, they were being attacked on a personal level.

Knowing this, it makes sense why Paul thought spiritual warfare along with spiritual weaponry was the most important point for the Ephesians to remember.

Related by the Blood of Jesus and Comrades in Battle

Coming back to Ephesians 6:10, we read, "Finally, my brethren…" This word "brethren" comes from a form of the Greek word *adelphos*, which means *brother*. In the Greek language, the word *adelphe*, or "sister," is the female version of the word "brother."

The word *delphus* describes the womb of a woman. When the letter "*a*" is placed at the front of the word, it describes *two or more who were born out of the same womb*. Every time we refer to someone as a brother or sister, we're saying, "You and I have been conceived from the same source. We have been born from the same place. We have been born from above, born from the womb of God. You and I are related through the blood of Jesus Christ. We are members of the same family."

The Greeks also used the word *adelphos* in a militaristic sense to describe *comrades in a battle*. The word was first popularized during the time of Alexander the Great. Tragically, he died at the age of 33, but before he died, he was already considered legendary as the greatest soldier who ever lived.

Even today, when speaking with military experts, they will say there has never been a greater military leader than Alexander the Great. Because he was such a renowned soldier and commander, most soldiers of that day desired to know Alexander personally or have an affiliation with him.

Occasionally, Alexander the Great would host a ceremony to distribute awards on a stage. He would stand on a platform and, one by one, call out the names of soldiers who had been faithful in battle. He could have referred to them as "fellow soldier," but instead he called them *adelphos*. Alexander would wrap his arm around his comrade and say, "We are comrades in battle. We have faced the same enemy. We have battled together." Alexander would then associate himself with those soldiers as being fellow comrades in battle.

This is when the Greek word *adelphos* first became popularized in the Greek language. By the time of the New Testament, it was common for people to call one another *brother* or *sister*. The people of the New Testament times understood the word "brother" to mean more than just patting someone on the back. Whenever someone would wrap their arms around someone and call them "brother" or "sister," they were in essence saying, "We have been born out of the same womb of God. We have both been born from above. Not only that, we are comrades in battle. We are both in the fight. We are in the trenches together fighting it out against the enemy."

No matter how many times a fellow believer gets knocked down, as long as he or she gets back up and continues to fight against the enemy, we should be proud to be affiliated with that individual. Our fellow comrades may have taken a few hits along the way, but if they are still plodding ahead, we need to wrap our arms around them and say, "You are exactly the kind of person I am proud to be affiliated with."

Think of someone today who you know has been struggling but is still fighting the good fight of faith. Why don't you take a moment to put your arm around that person's shoulder and say, "I am proud to be called your friend and brother" or, "I am proud to be your sister and friend."

Taking into account all the original Greek meanings of key words in this verse, here is the *Renner Interpretive Version (RIV)* of Ephesians 6:10:

> **Finally, to the last and most important matter at hand. I've saved the most important thing to the very end so that if you don't remember anything else, this will stay in your mind; this will stick with you, my brothers, my comrades in battle: Be strong in the Lord and in the power of His might**

A Command, Not a Suggestion

So what was Paul wanting to tell the Ephesians? "Be strong in the Lord, and in the power of His might" (Ephesians 6:10). This was actually a command, not a suggestion. Paul was writing like a general in the faith to people who were struggling in their personal lives. Paul was exhorting those he was addressing, "Hey guys, it's time for you to be strengthened and to be strong in the Lord."

If you determine to listen to what Paul said in this passage and open yourself to the Lord, He will gloriously fill you with all the strength you need to win any battle you are facing in your life today. He is faithful!

In the next lesson, we will delve even further into Ephesians 6:10!

STUDY QUESTIONS

**Study to shew thyself approved unto God, a workman that needeth
not to be ashamed, rightly dividing the word of truth.
— 2 Timothy 2:15**

1. In First Thessalonians 5:5, we are called "children of light." Explain this verse in light of John 8:12.
2. Define the Greek word *nepho*, translated as "sober." Explain why it is important to be "sober" during the days in which we are living. What are some ways we can remain sober and alert?
3. Paul described the breastplate and the helmet pieces from the armor of God differently in First Thessalonians 5:8 and Ephesians 6:14,17. Briefly explain the reason. Where does Paul's description of spiritual armor likely originate?

PRACTICAL APPLICATION

**But be ye doers of the word, and not hearers only,
deceiving your own selves.
— James 1:22**

1. Describe one weapon from the spiritual arsenal found in Ephesians 6 that you have recently utilized and the result. Can you think of a time when you used each weapon mentioned in Ephesians 6? Is there a weapon you have not utilized as much?

2. We are not supposed to stay stagnant in our knowledge and understanding of the Word of God. It is always good to take a moment and evaluate our growth and where we are in our walk with God. Are you growing in your understanding of the Word of God? What are some areas you have seen exponential growth over the last several years?

3. Read Second Samuel 23:9,10. Despite being tired, Eleazar held on to his sword in battle and God gave the victory. Compare this story to Ephesians 6:17 where Paul mentioned the "sword of the Spirit." Describe a time in your personal life when you held on to the Word of God and God gave you the victory.

4. Think of someone you know who has been struggling in a battle but is still fighting "the good fight of faith" (*see* 1 Timothy 6:12). Take a moment to pray and ask the Holy Spirit what you can do to bring encouragement to him or her.

LESSON 3

TOPIC

Power for the Fight

SCRIPTURES

1. **Ephesians 6:10** — Finally, my brethren, be strong in the Lord, and in the power of His might.

2. **Acts 1:8** — But ye shall receive power, after that the Holy Ghost is come upon you: and ye shall be witnesses unto me both in Jerusalem, and in all Judaea, and in Samaria, and unto the uttermost part of the earth.

3. **Luke 24:49** — And, behold, I send the promise of my Father upon you: but tarry ye in the city of Jerusalem, until ye be endued with power from on high.

GREEK WORDS

1. "Finally" — **Τοῦ λοιποῦ** (*Tou loipou*): to the last and most important matter at hand; for the rest of the matter; finally

2. "brother" or "sister" — ἀδελφός (*adelphos*) or ἀδελφὴ (*adelphe*): a term used to describe two or more who were born from the same womb; an endearing term used to describe those of one's own family; later used in a military sense to depict brothers in battle; a comrade; hence, brotherhood

3. "strong" — ἐνδύω (*enduo*): a compound of ἐν (*en*) and δύναμις (*dunamis*); the word ἐν (*en*) means into, such as in placing water into a vessel, and δύναμις (*dunamis*) means supernatural power; dynamic power; the word *dunamis* depicts the full might of an advancing army; it describes a force of nature like an earthquake, a tornado, or a hurricane; power that is to be placed inside something; this is not free-floating power in the universe; this is divine, supernatural, earth-shaking, hurricane-moving, tornado-blasting, army-force power that is placed inside an instrument or vessel; it pictures the power of a whole army being deposited into a person; inner strengthening; supernatural enablement; pictures explosive, superhuman power that comes with enormous energy and produces phenomenal, extraordinary, and unparalleled results being deposited into a receptacle

4. "behold" — ἰδού (*idou*): the idea of bewilderment, shock, amazement, or a loss of words

5. "power" — κράτος (*kratos*): demonstrated or eruptive power

6. "might" — ἰσχύς (*ischus*): might; man that is muscle-bound; a man covered in muscles; a strong man or a mighty man

A PROPHETIC WORD FROM THE LORD

A Storm Is Coming — Spiritual War!
Batten Down the Hatches!

We're headed into a season of intense warfare on many fronts — *economical*, *political*, and *spiritual*. But the Lord is a Man of War, and He knows exactly how to strategize against and overcome every assault against His people and against His Truth.

But just as one should batten down the hatches in a time of storms, God's people must be mentally and spiritually prepared for a stormy season that lies directly ahead. But with the grace of

God, the power of the Holy Spirit, the promises of God's Word, and the weaponry He has given, we can move forward step by step with the strategic guidance of the Holy Spirit. And God will triumphantly lead His people forward and will carry out His plans for this end-time age.

This is not a time to fear, moan, or cry, but a time to *rejoice*, for God is strategically at work even in ways that you do not see. Although it may seem the enemy and those he is influencing are derailing God's purposes, remember that the One who sits in the heavens laughs at their plans, and He will ultimately have them in derision (*see* Psalm 2:4). God is a Man of War, and in the end, His purposes shall surely prevail.

SYNOPSIS

We have been commanded to be strong in the Lord and in the power of His might. There are times in battle when we must "tough it out" and persevere through the fight. To do so, we need God's divine, supernatural, earthshaking, hurricane-moving, tornado-blasting, army-force, *dunamis* power. We have been created as containers for that power and must simply receive it. We have been provided supernatural weaponry to overcome the enemy, but to carry it we must receive the baptism in the Holy Spirit. We will be supernaturally connected to the power of God as a result.

The emphasis of this lesson:

By receiving the promise of the Father — the Holy Spirit — we become containers of God's power — the demonstrative, explosive, resurrecting, force-of-nature power of God. God specifically designed us to be receptacles of this earthshaking power. All we need to do is receive it. By receiving this power, we are transformed into superhuman beings, and this enables us to be clothed in the full armor of God to defeat the devil and his assaults against our lives!

Review of Lesson 2:
Born of the Same Womb

In the previous lesson, we began delving into Ephesians 6:10, which says, "Finally, my brethren, be strong in the Lord, and in the power of his might." In the Greek language, we have learned that the word "finally" means *to the last and most important matter at hand*. Essentially, Paul was saying, "I've saved this point until the end, so if you don't remember anything else, remember this."

We have also learned the word "brethren" is the Greek word *adelphos*, which means *brother*. In Greek, the word describes *two born out of the same womb or from the same source*. Those of us who are followers of Christ and have been reborn from the womb of God are born from above and are related by the blood of Jesus.

In the New Testament, the Greek word *adelphos* also militaristically describes comrades in battle. By referring to another believer as "brother" or "sister," we are acknowledging that we are fighting together in the trenches; we are comrades. When we are affiliated with another believer who seems to be struggling, but is still fighting, we need to be proud to be spiritually related to that individual.

The Command:
Be Strong in the Lord

Moving on to the next part of this verse, Ephesians 6:10 says, "Finally, my brethren, be strong in the Lord." In the Greek, this is not a suggestion; it is a command. We are commanded to be strong in the Lord. What does it mean to be strong in the Lord? Does it mean to just tough it out in ourselves? There are certainly times when we need to persevere through difficult circumstances confronting our lives, but without God's divine power, we will fail.

The word "strong" in this verse is the Greek word *enduo*. This word is a compound of two Greek words: *en* and *duo*. The word *en* means "in," as in *to be inside something*. The word *duo* is a form of the Greek word *dunamis*. The word *dunamis* describes *supernatural, dynamic power*. It was used in the First Century to describe the full might of an advancing army. Paul used this word to describe *a force of nature like an earthquake or tornado or hurricane*. This word refers to *an amazing, supernatural power like an earthquake to shake things up, like a tornado to blow things out of the way, like a hurricane to move in and change the entire environment*.

In Acts 1:8, Jesus said, "But ye shall receive power, after that the Holy Ghost is come upon you..." The Greek word for "power" in this verse is the same word *dunamis*, and it is showing that this is the kind of power we have received when the Holy Spirit came upon us. However, in Ephesians 6:10, it is not just *dunamis*; it is the compounded word *enduo*. When compounded, *enduo* is referring to this *dunamis* power being placed inside of something. It is not a free-floating power. It is a divine, supernatural, earthshaking, hurricane-moving, tornado-blasting, army-force power that is placed inside some type of instrument or vessel. Paul was speaking directly to *you*. This divine, *dunamis* power was designed to be placed on the inside of you. You are the receptacle chosen by God to hold that power. That is something to shout about!

Designed To Hold God's Divine Power

Another place we can find the words *enduo and dunamis* is in Luke 24:49, where Jesus was on the Mount of Olives preparing to ascend to Heaven. Jesus knew He was about to leave His followers and He said, "…Behold, I send the promise of my Father upon you: but tarry ye in the city of Jerusalem, until ye be endued with power from on high."

The Greek word for "behold," is *idou*, which carries *the idea of bewilderment, shock, amazement*, or *a loss of words*. By using the word "behold," Jesus was injecting His own sentiment into the text. He was essentially saying, "Wow! Wait until you hear this! This is amazing! This will leave you at a loss for words! Wow! Behold!"

But what was Jesus so excited about?

> **…Behold, I send the promise of my Father upon you: but tarry ye in the city of Jerusalem, until ye be *endued with power from on high*.**
> **— Luke 24:49**

Jesus was referring to the baptism in the Holy Spirit and describes it as an enduement. When you're filled with the Holy Spirit, you become the recipient of this divine power. It is what Jesus called "the promise of God." We can see this promise being fulfilled in Acts 2 when the Spirit of God came on the Day of Pentecost. Everyone in that room was filled with the Holy Ghost and spoke with other tongues. On that day, they each received this divine power.

Before, they were hiding behind doors for fear of the Jews. They were cowardly. But when this divine, *dunamis* power came in them — *enduo* — they were so empowered that they threw open those doors, emerged in the streets, and began preaching boldly. They were *transformed* by this power.

With this power, they had received the might of an army; the power of an earthquake to shake things up; the power of a tornado to blow things out of the way; the power of a hurricane to change the environment. They became a supernatural force of nature, and that's what *you* have access to as well!

If you've never received the power of God that I'm describing, please contact RENNER Ministries at 1-800-742-5593 and let us pray with you. If you are a child of God, you've been designed as a receptacle to hold this power, and God is waiting to fill you with the power of the Holy Spirit. It belongs to *you*.

In fact, the word *enduo* was used in classical Greek literature to describe individuals who suddenly received a touch from the gods they worshiped. Prior to this touch, these humans were deemed weaklings, but when the touch from the gods came upon them, they were transformed into super-human beings.

Similarly to what is described in classical Greek literature, when we are filled with the Holy Spirit, we are transformed from being weaklings into superhuman beings! We are literally transformed by the power of God!

The Seven Pieces of God's Weaponry

Returning to Ephesians 6:10, why did Paul begin this whole chapter with the subject of weapons and the power of the Holy Spirit? Paul described seven pieces of the spiritual weaponry available to every believer in a parallel comparison to the seven pieces of weaponry that make up the Roman soldier's armor.

The seven pieces of armor that the Roman soldiers of Paul's day wore includes the following:

1. His shoes and greaves
2. His belt
3. His breastplate
4. His sword
5. His shield
6. His helmet
7. His spear

When all these pieces were combined, this weaponry was *heavy*. In fact, this armor was so heavy, someone who was physically weak could not carry or function with them. If a person was physically weak, he wouldn't even be able to get out of his chair, let alone fight an impending enemy, clothed with these weapons. Only a person who was extremely strong could carry and operate with this level of weaponry.

So before Paul even got to the issue of weapons in Ephesians 6, he first dealt with the issue of power. It is the equivalent of saying, "I'm going to tell you about weapons, but before we get into that, I want to tell you about what you need in order to carry the weaponry."

You need to be endued with God's divine power. That power is essential if you're going to perform well in spiritual warfare and use all the weaponry God has provided.

The Eruptive Power of His Might

In Ephesians 6:10, Paul continued, "…Be strong in the Lord, and in the power of His might." What is the difference between "power" and "might" in this verse? In effect, the words "power of His might" describe the strength ascribed to us when this divine power is placed inside us.

In this passage in Ephesians 6:10, the words "power" and "might" have different meanings because they are two distinct words in the Greek language. The word "power" in this verse is the Greek word *kratos*. It describes *demonstrated or eruptive power*. This is not theoretical power or a something we mentally assent to and believe in; *it is demonstrated power!* It is observable and can be felt.

An example of this demonstrative, *kratos* power of God was when the earthquake shook the tomb where the body of Jesus was laid and the stone was rolled away. If you had been at the tomb that day, you would not have just mentally assented to the fact that Jesus had been resurrected; you would have actually felt that power. This was the *demonstrative, eruptive, kratos* power of God.

The Greek word for "might" is *ischus*. It describes a man who is muscle-bound. When this verse says "in the power of His might," it is talking about God's might or His muscles. Imagine if you could actually see the right arm of God, which is mentioned many times throughout the Scriptures. What do you think it would look like? No human that has ever existed could compare to the muscular *ischus* power of God. When we receive the baptism and infilling of the Holy Spirit, we receive this divine *ischus* power, supernaturally connecting us to the muscular ability of God.

When we pray in the name of Jesus and act in faith, God flexes His muscles, and *kratos* power — the *demonstrated eruptive power* of God — occurs in an observable way. When that power manifests, it drives out enemies, brings forth signs and wonders, and changes the atmosphere and landscape around us. This all happens when we receive this power from God.

We have been fashioned by God as receptacles of His power and before we are able to carry the spiritual weapons at our disposal, we must receive the *kratos* and *ischus* power of God through the baptism in the Holy Spirit!

If you have never received this power, call RENNER Ministries at 1-800-742-5593, and we will pray with you!

STUDY QUESTIONS

Study to shew thyself approved unto God, a workman that needeth not to be ashamed, rightly dividing the word of truth.
— 2 Timothy 2:15

1. Describe how the word "brethren" (*adelphos*) was used by soldiers in ancient Rome and what it meant to them. How does this use of *adelphos* affect how you see fellow believers?

2. Explain the meaning of the Greek word *enduo* and its importance to born-again believers.

3. Consider Acts 2. After the believers who were waiting in the Upper Room received the *enduo* power of God on the Day of Pentecost, what was the immediate result? Now read Acts 19:1-6 and describe the result of the believers in Ephesus receiving the *enduo* power of God into their lives. What are the similarities between these two passages? Have you ever had a similar experience with the infilling of the Holy Spirit?

PRACTICAL APPLICATION

> But be ye doers of the word, and not hearers only,
> deceiving your own selves.
> —James 1:22

1. Think about a time when a brother or sister in the Lord brought you encouragement during a time of spiritual battle. Now take a moment to think about someone you know who might need your prayer support. Allow the Holy Spirit to lead you. Pray for those that have helped you in your time of need and pray for those who may need *your* support.

2. If you are born again (*see* Romans 10:8-10) but have not received the power Jesus promised in Luke 24:49 and Acts 1:8, take a moment to receive this gift or call RENNER Ministries at 1-800-742-5593, and a specially trained prayer partner will pray with you.

3. Reflect on a time when you have walked in your own might to resolve a battle. What was the result? How did that compare to allowing God's might to manifest in the fight? Why is it important to be strong in the Lord and the power of His might instead of our own power and might?

LESSON 4

TOPIC

How To Put on the Whole Armor of God

SCRIPTURES

1. **1 Timothy 1:18** — This charge I commit unto thee, son Timothy, according to the prophecies which went before on thee, that thou by them mightiest war a good warfare.

2. **Ephesians 6:10,11** — Finally, my brethren, be strong in the Lord, and in the power of his might. Put on the whole armour of God, that ye may be able to stand against the wiles of the devil.

3. **Ephesians 6:13,14** — Wherefore take unto you the whole armour of God, that ye may be able to withstand in the evil day, and having done all, to stand. Stand therefore, having your loins girt about with truth, and having on the breastplate of righteousness.

GREEK WORDS

1. "put on" — ἐνδύω (*enduo*): compound of ἐν (*en*) and δύναμις (*dunamis*); the word ἐν (*en*) means into, such as in placing water into a vessel, and δύναμις (*dunamis*) means supernatural power; dynamic power; the word *dunamis* depicts the full might of an advancing army; it describes a force of nature like an earthquake, a tornado, or a hurricane; power that is to be placed inside something; this is not free-floating power in the universe; this is divine, supernatural, earth-shaking, hurricane-moving, tornado-blasting, army-force power that is placed inside an instrument or vessel; it pictures the power of a whole army being deposited into a person; inner strengthening; supernatural enablement; pictures explosive, superhuman power that comes with enormous energy and produces phenomenal, extraordinary, and unparalleled results being deposited into a receptacle

2. "be strong" — ἐνδύω (*enduo*): compound of ἐν (en) and δύναμις (*dunamis*); the word ἐν (*en*) means into, such as in placing water into a vessel, and δύναμις (*dunamis*) means supernatural power; dynamic power; the word dunamis depicts the full might of an advancing army; it describes a force of nature like an earthquake, a tornado, or a hurricane; power that is to be placed inside something; this is not free-floating power in the universe; this is divine, supernatural, earth-shaking, hurricane-moving, tornado-blasting, army-force power that is placed inside an instrument or vessel; it pictures the power of a whole army being deposited into a person; inner strengthening; supernatural enablement; pictures explosive, superhuman power that comes with enormous energy and produces phenomenal, extraordinary, and unparalleled results being deposited into a receptacle

3. "power" — κράτος (*kratos*): demonstrated or eruptive power

4. "might" — ἰσχύς (*ischus*): might; man that is muscle-bound; a man covered in muscles; a strong man or a mighty man

5. "take unto you" — ἀναλάβετε (*analabete*): a compound of ἀνά (ana), which means to repeat an action over again, and λάβετε (labete), meaning to actively receive; together, it means to do it like you once

did; gives the image of the armor of God laying on the floor around you as if it had fallen off

6. "whole armour" — πανοπλία (*panoplia*): compound of πᾶν (*pan*), meaning all, and ὅπλον (*hoplon*), which is the Greek word for weaponry; together, it means absolutely all the weaponry God has provided; pictures a soldier fully dressed in his armor from head to toe; the full attire and weaponry of a soldier; the following hardware was required for a soldier to be fully dressed for battle: the loinbelt, breastplate, shoes, shield, helmet, sword, and lance.

SYNOPSIS

There are many battles being waged in our world today. Fear, intimidation, and discouragement are rampant and are even affecting born-again believers. But God's Word provides many spiritual weapons and when we access those weapons, the devil can't win! Paul exhorted Timothy to "wage war" against the devil through the prophecies he had been given. Believers today can do the same. As receptacles of God's power, we have been designed by God to receive and operate in that power. God has instructed us, His followers, to "put on" the full armor of God, and when we do, the enemy no longer sees us — he sees God!

The emphasis of this lesson:

The armor of God is essential to living a victorious life in Christ. We must "put on" the weapons God has made available to us. By being endued with power by the infilling of the Holy Spirit, we are equipped to be clothed with the full armor of God.

Enemy-Defeating Weapons

Paul exhorted Timothy in First Timothy 1:18, "This charge I commit unto thee, son Timothy, according to the prophecies which went before on thee, that thou by them mightest war a good warfare." Just like Timothy, we can use prophecy as a weapon against the attacks of the enemy. In order to defeat the enemy, we need to have knowledge of the weapons available to us. We already know our enemy is not going to be victorious over our lives because God will fulfill His purposes in society, in all the nations, in our lives, and in our family's lives. But God has also given us weapons so *we* can do our part to walk in victory.

In the last several lessons, we have been studying Ephesians 6:10 where Paul recorded a teaching about the enemy, spiritual weaponry, and spiritual warfare for the church of Ephesus' benefit that also applies to our lives today. In this lesson, we will move on to verse 11.

> **Finally, my brethren, be strong in the Lord, and in the power of his might.** *Put on the full armour of God,* **that ye may be able to stand against the wiles of the devil.**
> — Ephesians 6:10,11

Notice the first part of verse 11: "Put on the full armor of God...." This begs the question, "How do we put on the whole armor of God?" Some people figuratively put on armor when they wake up in the morning. They go through the motions of putting on a breastplate, helmet, belt, and shoes. They take their imaginary shield, sword, and spear. But just going through such gyrations does not dress you in anything. It's just a practice some people go through to remind themselves of what God has given them.

So how *do* we put on the armor of God? The answer is found in the Greek word for "put on," which is *enduo*. Do you recognize that word? It is the same word used in verse 10 for "be strong!" The word *enduo* is a compound word comprised of the Greek words *en*, meaning *in* as in *to be inside something*, and *duo*, which is a derivative of *dunamis*. God's *dunamis* power describes *dynamic, supernatural power*. It describes *the full might of an advancing army* or *a force of nature like a hurricane or tornado or earthquake.* God's *dunamis* power is supernatural and is like a one-man army.

When the Greek words *en* and *duo* are combined, it is the Greek word *enduo*. This word means *to be strong*, and it pictures taking this divine power and putting it into some type of container. You are the receptacle God created to hold His power. This power is not intended to be a free-floating power that drifts through the atmosphere. God intended for it to be put in a receptacle, and that is you! In fact, you should wrap your arms around yourself and say, "I am the container for the power of God!" That is what this word actually means.

Ephesians 6:10 tells us that when this power is received, it makes us strong in the Lord and in the power of His might. Once again, the word "power" in this verse is *kratos*, describing *a demonstrated, eruptive power*. It is a power that can be seen and felt, and it produces signs and wonders. Then the word "might" is the Greek word *ischus*, and it describes someone who is muscle-bound like a bodybuilder. But in this verse "His might" is describing God's might. There is no one who can compare to the muscular ability of God. When we receive the power of God through the baptism in the Holy Spirit, we are filled with a power that divinely connects us to the muscular ability of God Himself.

There is no one that can compare with the muscular ability of God. While on earth, when we pray in the name of Jesus or walk in faith, God flexes His muscles, His *ischus*, and that power is released through us and shows up as signs and wonders — *demonstrated, eruptive power.*

When people are baptized in the Holy Spirit, they often have a sudden urge to do something supernatural. The power of the Holy Spirit in them wants to manifest and erupt. Suddenly, there is a desire to cast out demons, heal the sick, and demonstrate something supernatural because of God's power now residing on the inside.

The Power That Dresses Us In God's Weaponry

As we have learned in the previous lessons, Paul began his discourse in Ephesians 6 with the subject of power because the weapons described in Ephesians 6 were very heavy. A weakling could not carry or function in these weapons. Only a very strong soldier could carry and operate in these seven pieces of weaponry. Without the strength needed to carry it, no man would be able to run or fight their enemy while bearing the weight of all that armor. The same is true with spiritual weaponry — it takes the power of the Holy Spirit inside us to wield those spiritual weapons. That is the reason when discussing the subject of weaponry, we must begin with the question of power. If you've never received the baptism in the Holy Spirit, you can receive it by simply asking God. If you call RENNER Ministries at 800-742-5593, we will pray with you, and you will receive this supernatural power.

Ephesians 6:11 says we are to "put on the whole armor of God." The Greek word for "put on" is *enduo*, meaning that when we receive the supernatural power of God, it is that same power that dresses us in the weaponry Paul was describing. As long as we are walking in that power, it puts a helmet on our head and a breastplate on our chest, and it wraps a loin belt around us. The power of God puts greaves on our shins and shoes on our feet. His power also puts a shield in one hand and a sword in the other. And that same power of God gives us a spear to use for long-distance attacks against the enemy. As long as we continue to walk in the power of God, we are dressed in all of the weaponry God provides.

Refilled With His Power

Continuing in Ephesians 6:13 and 14, Paul said, "Wherefore take unto you the whole armour of God, that ye may be able to withstand in the evil day, and having done all, to stand. Stand therefore, having your loins girt about with truth, and having on the breastplate of righteousness."

The phrase "take unto you" in Greek is *analibete*. The word *ana* means *to repeat the action*, and *libete* means *to receive the action*. When these two words are combined, *analibete* means *do it like you once did it*, but pictures someone with the armor of God, but it's scattered on the floor all around him. This tells us that the Ephesian believers had dropped their weaponry.

Ephesians chapter four describes those believers walking in strife, bitterness, and wrath. They were backbiting, lying, and stealing. In fact, their behavior was so awful, they were actually grieving the Holy Spirit. The believers Paul was addressing were not behaving like people walking in the power of God. Similarly, when we step away from the power of God, our spiritual armor begins to fall off all around us — even though it is legally ours.

But there is some good news! If we have laid down our armor, we can pick it back up and put it on again by asking the Lord to refill us with His power.

Putting On the Full Armor of God

Verse 11 says, "Put on the whole armour of God." The words "put on" actually means that when we are endued with the power of God, that power begins to completely outfit us in the "whole armor of God." In Greek, the words "whole armor" comes from a form of *panoplia*. The word *pan* means *all of it*, and *oplia* is derived from the word *hoplon*, meaning *all the weapons*. When these words are compounded, it means *absolutely all the weaponry that God has provided.*

On page 181 of Rick's book *Dressed To Kill*, it says:

> That phrase [whole armor] is taken from the Greek word *panoplia*, and it refers to *a Roman soldier who is fully dressed in his armor from head to toe.* Since this is the example Paul puts before us, we have to consider the full dress, the *panoplia*, of the

Roman soldier…. Paul could see the Roman soldier's *loinbelt; huge breastplate; brutal shoes affixed with spikes; massive, full-length shield; intricate helmet; piercing sword;* and *long, specially tooled lance….*

Number One: Loinbelt

First of all, the Roman soldier wore *a loinbelt.* Although it was the least impressive and most commonplace piece of weaponry that the Roman soldier wore, *it was the central piece of armor that held all the other parts together.*

Number Two: Breastplate

The Roman soldier also wore a second weapon — *a magnificent and beautiful breastplate.* The breastplate of the Roman soldier was made out of two large sheets of metal. One piece covered the front of the soldier, and the other piece covered his back; then these two sheets of metal were attached at the top of the soldier's shoulders by large brass rings…. This heavy piece of weaponry began at the bottom of the neck and extended down past the waist to the knees.

Number Three: Shoes

In addition…the Roman soldier also wore *a pair of very dangerous shoes….* Beginning right at the top of the knee, [the Roman shoe] extended down past the calf of the leg and rested on top of the foot…. On the bottom, the Roman soldier's shoes were affixed with extremely dangerous spikes. These shoes, which Paul amazingly calls 'shoes of peace' in Ephesians 6:15, were intended to be 'killer shoes.'

Number Four: Shield

The Roman soldier also carried a fourth important weapon — *a large, oblong shield.* This massive shield was made of multiple layers of animal hide that were tightly woven together and then framed along the edges by a strong piece of metal or wood.

Number Five: Helmet

The fifth weapon that the Roman soldier wore was his *helmet*. This all-important piece of armor, which protected the soldier from receiving a fatal blow to the head, sometimes weighed 15 pounds or more. Whereas the breastplate was the most beautiful piece of weaponry the Roman soldier possessed, the helmet was the most noticeable.

Number Six: Sword

The sixth weapon of the Roman soldier was his *sword*. Although there were many kinds of swords during that time in history, the sword the Roman soldier carried was one specifically designed for thrusting to inflict a deadly wound on an adversary or foe.

Number Seven: Lance

Finally, the Roman soldier also carried a seventh weapon — *a specially tooled lance* designed to strike the enemy from a distance.

All of these were essential pieces of weaponry used by every Roman or Greek soldier at the time Paul wrote this description. The word *panoplia* is used in Ephesians 6:11 and 13 to describe all the weapons in our arsenal of spiritual weaponry and armament. God has given all believers every one of the weapons described here by Paul.

How To Look Like God

Again, Ephesians 6:11 says, "Put on the whole armour of God, that ye may be able to stand against the wiles of the devil." The Greek language describes these weapons as coming out of God, but the tense used also means that when we are dressed in this weaponry, we actually look like God!

Think about Jesus. He lived in Nazareth for the first 30 years of His life. Not one time during those 30 years did a single demon cry out, "I know you! You are the Holy One of God!" Not even one. But after Jesus was baptized in the Holy Spirit and received the power of God at the river Jordan, as He walked home on the very same streets of Nazareth He had walked on His entire life, the response toward Him changed.

People that were demon possessed began screaming, "I know you. I know who You are. You're the Holy One of God!"

What did those demons see that they had not seen before? Jesus looked the same: His hair was the same, His clothing was the same, His appearance was the same. So what changed? When Jesus was baptized in the Holy Spirit, He was clothed with the whole armor of God, and now, in the spirit realm, He looked different. The demons were seeing Him in the Spirit.

Now when Jesus walked down the same streets, the demons began shrieking with terror because they saw Him dressed in the whole armor of God.

When you receive the power of God and are dressed from head to toe with God's armor, it changes you spiritually. The enemy sees you and becomes terrified! When you are fully dressed in the armor of God, you actually look like God Himself, and the devil runs in terror! This is the value of being clothed in the spiritual weapons God has made available to you. It all begins by receiving the power of God through the infilling of the Holy Spirit.

In our next lesson, we will learn the five words of warfare so we can recognize the devil's war tactics and be better prepared for any battles ahead.

STUDY QUESTIONS

Study to shew thyself approved unto God, a workman that needeth not to be ashamed, rightly dividing the word of truth.
— 2 Timothy 2:15

1. Merely going through the motions of putting on the armor of God does not actually clothe us in His spiritual armor. So how *can* we put on the armor of God? Describe the prerequisite to spiritually putting on the whole armor of God and explain the reason it is necessary.

2. Define the meaning of the Greek word *ischus*. Explain how we connect to the *ischus* power of God and the results of that connection.

3. Read First Samuel 17:38-40 and explain the reason David could not bear the armor that did not belong to him. How does this compare to our spiritual lives? What is necessary for us to bear the spiritual armor of God?

PRACTICAL APPLICATION

But be ye doers of the word, and not hearers only,
deceiving your own selves.
—James 1:22

1. Explain First Timothy 1:18 in your own words. As part of this series, Rick has shared his own word from the Lord. How can this word prepare you for whatever storms may come this next year? How else can you apply this verse to your life in the future?
2. Reflect on a time when you dropped your spiritual weaponry. What was the catalyst for this? Have you retrieved those weapons? What are some steps you can take to prevent dropping your spiritual weaponry again?
3. Identify an area in your life where the enemy has been relentless in his attack (health, finances, relationships, etc.). Find at least two verses to cling to as you wield the sword of the Spirit, defeating the enemy. Record the date when that victory manifests.

LESSON 5

TOPIC

Five Words of Warfare

SCRIPTURES

1. **Ephesians 6:10,11** — Finally, my brethren, be strong in the Lord, and in the power of his might. Put on the whole armour of God, that ye may be able to stand against the wiles of the devil.
2. **2 Corinthians 2:11** — Lest Satan should get and advantage of us: for we are not ignorant of his devices.
3. **2 Corinthians 10:4, 5** — (for the weapons of our warfare are not carnal, but mighty through God to the pulling down of strong holds;) Casting down imaginations, and every high thing that exalteth itself against the knowledge of God, and bringing into captivity every thought to the obedience of Christ.

4. **Acts 10:38** — How God anointed Jesus of Nazareth with the Holy Ghost and with power: who went about doing good, and healing all that were oppressed of the devil; for God was with him.

GREEK WORDS

1. "that ye may be able" — **δύναμαι** (dunamai): empowered; enabled; derived from **δύναμις** (*dunamis*), which is the idea of explosive, super-human power that comes with enormous energy and produces phe-nomenal, extraordinary, and unparalleled results; depicts the full might of an advancing army; describes a force of nature like an earthquake, a tornado, or a hurricane

2. "devil" — **διάβολος** (*diabolos*): a compound of the preposition **διά** (*dia*), which carries the idea of penetration, to go from one side all the way through to the other side; and **βάλλω** (*ballos*), meaning to strike or throw something like a ball or rock over and over again; combined, **διάβολος** (*diablos*) describes the way in which the devil operates; char-acteristic of the devil; one who repetitiously strikes until successfully penetrating an object to ruin it, affect it, or take it captive; to slander, accuse, or defame; to penetrate by continuous assault; to ensnare with a net

3. "wiles" — **μεθοδεία** (*methodeias*): a compound of the preposition **μετά** (*meta*), meaning with, and **ὁδός** (*hodos*), which is the word for a road, or an avenue, a path; combined, **μεθοδεία** (*methodeias*) describes one who operates with or travels on a road

4. "devices" — **νόημα** (*noemata*): a derivative of the word **νοῦς** (*nous*), the Greek word for the mind; the form **νόημα** (*noemata*) pictures a mind that is confused

5. "stong holds" — **ὀχύρωμα** (*ochuroma*): castle; fortress; citadel; pictures a stronghold with walls fortified to keep outsiders on the outside; a dreadful prison constructed deep inside a fortress that was intended to prevent a hostage or prisoner from escaping; a prison that holds a prisoner captive; a place of arrest, captivity, confinement, detention, imprisonment, or incarceration

6. "oppressed" — **καταδυναστεύω** (*katadunasteuo*): depicts a dominat-ing tyrant who lords himself over his subjects; pictures the oppressive power of a wicked tyrant; depicts one who rules over and cruelly tyrannizes his subjects; bullying; cruelty; despotism; dictatorship; oppressiveness; tyranny

SYNOPSIS

There are five words that enable us, through our understanding of their Greek definitions, to know how the devil tries to influence our thinking: 1) devil, 2) wiles, 3) devices, 4) strongholds, and 5) oppression. By gaining a deeper understanding of these words, we will learn to recognize his tactics of war against us and annihilate his plan for our defeat.

The emphasis of this lesson:

Satan has well-planned strategies to build strongholds in our thinking with the goal of making us prisoners of his lies. But God has provided us with His supernatural armor enabling us to stand strong against every attack!

Clothed in the Power of God

In our previous lessons, we have learned that by walking in the power of God, we put on the whole armor of God. The power of God dresses us from head to toe with His weapons. As long as we continue to walk in God's divine power, we are supernaturally outfitted with all kinds of spiritual weaponry. This weaponry comes out of God — it emanates from Him — and it operates in and by the power of God.

When the power of God hits you, it begins to clothe you. When that happens, the Greek implies that you begin to look like God to the enemy. A good example of this is Jesus.

For the first 30 years of Jesus' life, He never worked one miracle. He was a good man, but not one demon screamed out that knew who He was as He walked the streets of Nazareth. In fact, He didn't receive a single demonic reaction during those first 30 years.

But one day, Jesus went to the river Jordan where He was baptized by John the Baptist. It was at that moment that the Holy Spirit came upon Him and Jesus was endued with power from on High. Jesus received the baptism in the Holy Spirit, and when that power hit Jesus, it supernaturally clothed Him with divine weaponry.

We know Jesus was clothed in God's armor because for the first time in 30 years, when He went home to Nazareth where He had always lived, demons began reacting and seemed to "come out of the woodwork." They were screaming, "I know who You are! You are the Holy One of God. Don't torment us!"

Outwardly, Jesus was wearing the same clothes He had always worn and was walking on the same streets He had always walked on. His physical appearance hadn't changed. Everything in the physical realm was the same as before. So what *did* change? Something changed *spiritually*. The Holy Spirit came upon Him at the Jordan River and endued Him with power that equipped Him in spiritual armor. So in the spiritual realm, when Jesus returned home to Nazareth, He looked like a mighty warrior walking through the streets. The demons saw Him and began shrieking. They knew exactly who He was, and they were terrified!

This same thing happens when you receive the infilling of the Holy Spirit. You are endued with power from on High and outfitted with mighty spiritual weaponry — weaponry that absolutely terrifies the enemy.

In fact, it terrifies the enemy so much that Ephesians 6:11 goes on to say, "Put on the whole armor of God, that ye may be able *to stand against the wiles of the devil.*" The Greek word for "able" is *dunamai*, which gives this verse the following meaning: "…that you may be *empowered* to stand against the wiles of the devil."

Because we have been given the upper hand against the devil through the weapons God has given us, we can literally *push against* the wiles of the devil!

The Five Words of Warfare

But what *are* the wiles of the devil? By looking at several verses in Scripture, we can pinpoint five words in Greek that completely explain how the devil affects our thoughts and negatively influences our lives. By understanding these five words, you can stop the devil from oppressing and infiltrating your mind and ultimately controlling our lives.

1. 'Devil'

The name "devil" found in Ephesians 6:11 is from a form of the Greek word *diabolos*. It is a compound of two words: The first word is *dia*, a preposition that carries the idea of *penetration from one side all the way to the other side.* The second part of the word is *ballo*, which means *to throw like a ball or rock* or *to assault something.*

When compounded, we can conclude that the name "devil" or *diabolos* is actually a job description. It describes one who comes to assault. He comes equipped with deceitful, lying allegations. Just like a ball or rock, he is throwing and repeatedly hurling that lie. He is alleging and alleging with the goal to penetrate our thoughts. The devil will strike and strike until he finally penetrates the mind from one side all the way to the other.

The devil understands that the mind is the control center of our life. We choose what to believe and what not to believe with our mind, and whoever controls our mind will ultimately control our life. If someone can control what we think, that individual can control our self-image. If someone can control our self-image, he can control how we project ourselves to others. Whoever controls our mind, controls *us*.

This is the reason educators want your mind. It's why Hollywood wants your mind. It's the reason the political system wants your mind. Everyone in all spheres of society is after your mind because these entities understand that if they have your mind, they have *you*!

2. 'Wiles'

The second word we are covering in this lesson is "wiles." The Greek word for "wiles" is *methodeias*, and it is also a compound word. The word *meta* means *with*, and the word *hodos* is the Greek word for *a road* or *an avenue*. When these two words are combined, it reveals that the devil actually has a sense of direction when he attacks. He is not randomly moving — he is specifically headed to his destination to ambush our thoughts. The devil operates *with a road* or an avenue of attack. He is headed directly for your thoughts, or mind, because he wants to seize your mind and then take it captive.

When the devil arrives at his destination, his goal is to pound and pound our thoughts with lies and accusations until he successfully penetrates the mind through and through — from one side all the way to the other side.

3. 'Devices'

Paul mentioned the third word in Second Corinthians 2:11, which says, "Lest Satan should get an advantage of us: for we are not ignorant of his devices."

The word "devices" is the Greek word *noemata*. The word *noema* is a derivative of the Greek word *nous*. This word *nous* is the word for *mind*. But when *nous* becomes *noema*, it no longer refers only to a mind; it describes *a mind that is messed up*. It pictures *a brain that becomes so scrambled it can no longer think correctly*.

The devil's intention is to pound and pound until he finally knocks a hole into the mind, paving a road into our thoughts until he has penetrated from one side to the other. His goal is to so completely infiltrate our mind with his lies that our thoughts become scrambled, and we can no longer think or see things correctly in life — so much so that all we would hear are voices telling us what to think and feel, which would only result in confused thinking.

4. 'Strongholds'

Our fourth word, "strongholds," can be found in Second Corinthians 10:4, where Paul said, "for the weapons of our warfare are not carnal, but mighty through God to the pulling down of strong holds." The word "strongholds" is a very ancient Greek word depicting two different ideas. The first describes a castle or a fortress; the second describes a prison holding a prisoner captive. A stronghold that refers to a castle or fortress pictures something with very tall, thick walls designed to keep outsiders out. But a stronghold that refers to a prison pictures something that has the opposite effect; this kind of stronghold is designed to keep a captive on the inside.

Once the devil has pounded his way into a person's brain and confused his thinking — distorting the way he sees, thinks, and perceives — he starts building a stronghold in the person's mind. Once that stronghold is formed, it keeps the person trapped like a prisoner inside his or her wrong thinking so those who are trying to help can't penetrate those thick walls of lies. But it's all an imagination.

Second Corinthians 10:5 continues, "Casting down imaginations, and every high thing that exalteth itself against the knowledge of God, and bringing into captivity every thought to the obedience of Christ." When a person has allowed the enemy to infiltrate his or her mind with his lying thoughts or imaginations, the devil makes that person a prisoner of something that is imaginary. The lies he used to penetrate the person's thoughts are not real, but they feel real because his or her thoughts have become confused. Many believers are living behind these imaginary prison bars, thinking and believing they will never be free — when, in fact, they are already free. *Jesus died to set them free!*

Again, the devil's goal is to build a lie in our thinking that is so well-fortified that we will not see ourselves, our situation, or others accurately, and he can just move in to tyrannize us and take control. He wants to dominate our brain and control our emotions. He wants to dictate what we will feel and what we will believe about ourselves. Once that lie has been built up and fortified in our thoughts, he will — like a tyrant — sit on the throne of our mind and dominate us!

5. 'Oppression'

This brings us to the last word that describes how the devil wages war against us, and it can be found in Acts 10:38, which says, "How God anointed Jesus of Nazareth with the Holy Ghost and with power: who went about doing good, and healing all that were oppressed of the devil; for God was with him." The Greek word for "oppressed" is a form of *katadunasteuo*, which describes *a tyrant*. Typically, a tyrant lives in a castle and, from his lofty position, lords himself over his subjects.

Taking this image into account, Acts 10:38 could be translated, "Jesus was anointed with the Holy Ghost and with power: who went about doing good and healing all who were being tyrannized and terrorized by the devil."

The devil's goal for your life is to build a lie in your head that is so well-fortified, he can move right in. He wants to sit on the throne of your mind. He wants to control your emotions and dictate what you feel and believe about yourself. He is an absolute tyrant. If allowed, he will eventually tell you what to think and what not to think; what to believe and what not to believe; what you are going to earn and what you will never earn; what your future holds and what your future will never be; what your marriage will be and what it will never be. He will dominate you like a tyrant if he is permitted to do it.

Understanding the Devil's Five Strategies Will Give You the Upper Hand

If we understand the five words we just reviewed, we will basically understand how the devil finds access into a person's mind and entire life if he or she allows it. If we can understand all the devil's strategies, we won't be taken off guard when he uses them against us!

Here are those five words in review:

1. Devi (*diablos*) — one who repetitiously strikes with the goal of complete and total penetration.
2. Wiles (*methodeias*) — one who operates with or travels on a road.
3. Devices (*noemata*) — a mind that is totally confused.
4. Strongholds (*ochuroma*) — a place of arrest, captivity, confinement, detention, imprisonment, or incarceration.
5. Oppression (*katadunasteuo*) — a dominating tyrant.

The devil will strike you again and again until he achieves total penetration into your mind, where he will try to rule your entire life. He only operates in one lane and toward one purpose — to dominate your mind. Once he manages to get in your head, his goal is to scramble your mind until you're totally confused. And be warned: What you listen to consistently is what you will eventually believe. The devil will keep feeding you lies, and if you keep listening to those lies, you will one day believe them. That misplaced faith will only empower those lies and will create a stronghold in your mind, imprisoning you with something that is imaginary. Then, like a tyrant, the devil will move into your head and dominate you for the rest of your life — unless you pull down those lies and imaginations and destroy them!

Understanding these five words of warfare and how the devil operates will help you recognize his strategy and stop his assault at any point along the way. The armor of God gives you the upper hand so you can stand against every attack. Instead of retreating, you can push back against the wiles of the devil.

When we are dressed in the whole armor of God, it stops the devil from finding an entrance into our life. If he crosses a line into our space, we have everything we need to push him back across the line. God has given us divine weapons!

STUDY QUESTIONS

Study to shew thyself approved unto God, a workman that needeth
not to be ashamed, rightly dividing the word of truth.
— 2 Timothy 2:15

1. How can we walk in the whole armor of God, and what enables us to be clothed in that armor?
2. How did Jesus' life change after He received the baptism of the Holy Spirit? How did demons act before the Baptism and after? Why did they act differently? What can we take from this example of Jesus being endued with power from on High?
3. Explain in your own words the meaning of "whoever controls your mind controls you."
4. List the five words associated with warfare and write a brief description of each.

PRACTICAL APPLICATION

But be ye doers of the word, and not hearers only,
deceiving your own selves.
— James 1:22

1. If you have been baptized in the Holy Spirit, explain the difference this experience has made in your life. Give at least one example.
2. Have you ever experienced an assault on your mind? What happened and how did you overcome the enemy's persistent attacks? Would you change anything about how you handled previous attacks? If so, how would you overcome such attacks in the future?
3. Have you battled against a persistent lie in your life? Identify the lie. Take a few moments to pray in the Spirit and ask the Holy Spirit to give you a scripture to use as a weapon against that lie so you can hide that word in your heart and begin declaring it.

TOPIC

Unseen Spiritual Forces

SCRIPTURES

1. **Ephesians 6:12** — For we wrestle not against flesh and blood, but against principalities, against powers, against the rulers of the darkness of this world, against spiritual wickedness in high places.

GREEK WORDS

1. "wrestle" — πάλη (*pale*): intense conflict; struggling, wrestling, or slugging it out; hand-to-hand fighting; also the word from which the Greeks derived the word *Palaestra*, a famous house of combat sports, which included boxing, wrestling, and *pankration*

2. "not" — οὐκ (*ouk*): emphatically not; the strongest and most emphatic form of "no"

3. "against" — πρός (*pros*): an intimate encounter; being face to face with someone; pictures very close contact

4. "principalities" — ἀρχὰς (*archas*): chief, principal, or top rulers; where we get the word "archbishop"; refers to high-ranking demon spirits who hold the highest seats of power

5. "powers" — ἐξουσίας (*exousias*): those who have received delegated power; often translated "authority"; here it describes a sub-level of demons who have received license to exercise their dark influence wherever they wish to demonstrate it

6. "rulers of the darkness of this world" — κοσμοκράτορας (*kosmokratoras*): a compound of κόσμος (*kosmos*), which describes something that is ordered, and κράτος (*kratos*), meaning power; together, it pictures power that has been highly organized or disciplined; used in the First Century to describe taking the raw power of young men and training them as soldiers — organizing them, disciplining them, and harnessing that raw power into a powerful force that is then dispatched

7. "wickedness" — πονηρός (*poneros*): insidious, malevolent, or wicked

8. "high places" — ἐπουρανίοις (*epouraniois*): the atmosphere in which humans live; the air below the mountaintops or the air that we breathe

SYNOPSIS

The devil is organized, disciplined, and committed to his cause, but are we? Ephesians 6:12 tells us that we are not wrestling against flesh and blood, but against principalities, powers, rulers of the darkness of this world, and spiritual wickedness. These are the unseen forces coming against us. But the power of God within us is so much greater than any power the devil and his dark forces can ever hurl against us. We just need to stay committed to fight until the very end!

The emphasis of this lesson:

The enemy has arrayed his evil forces against all born-again believers. Understanding his tactics through the mindset of the ancient Greeks reveals how fierce the enemy is in his attacks against the Body of Christ. But God has given us His spiritual weaponry to come through every battle victorious!

A PROPHETIC WORD FROM THE LORD

A Storm Is Coming — Spiritual War!
Batten down the hatches!

We are headed into a season of intense warfare on many fronts — *economic*, *political*, and *spiritual*. But the Lord is a Man of War, and He knows exactly how to strategize against and overcome every assault against His people and against His Truth.

But just as one should batten down the hatches in a time of storms, God's people must be mentally and spiritually prepared for a stormy season that lies directly ahead. But with the grace of God, the power of the Holy Spirit, the promises of God's Word, and the weaponry He has given, we can move forward step by step with the strategic guidance of the Holy Spirit. And God will triumphantly lead His people forward and carry out His plans for this end-time age.

This is not a time to fear, moan, or cry, but a time to *rejoice*, for God is strategically at work even in ways you do not see. Although it may seem the enemy and those he is influencing are derailing God's purposes, remember that the One who sits in the heavens laughs at their plans, and He will ultimately have them in derision (*see* Psalm 2:4). God is a Man of War, and in the end, His purposes shall surely prevail.

Intense Conflict Against Unseen Evil Forces

In our two previous lessons, we focused on Ephesians 6:10 and 11 where we examined the power God has provided for you and me and how to put on the whole armor of God. We also learned about the five most important words we need to understand when it comes to the subject of spiritual warfare.

In this lesson, we'll be looking at the unseen evil forces we are up against, beginning in Ephesians 6:12, where Paul said, "For we wrestle not against flesh and blood, but *against* principalities, *against* powers, *against* the rulers of the darkness of this world, *against* spiritual wickedness in high places."

The King James Version of this verse very simply says, "For we wrestle," but the Greek has a much deeper meaning behind it. The word "wrestle" in Greek is *pale*, which describes *an intense conflict*. It means *to struggle, to really fight*, or *to slug it out*. It means *to really wrestle with unseen spiritual forces*. But there is something important in this verse that is not evident to us today. The readers in Paul's time were Greeks and Romans who read Greek and understood the culture of their day. When they read the word "wrestle," very distinct images flooded their minds.

Palaestra:
The House of Combat Sports

The Greeks and Romans in Paul's time understood that the Greek word for "wrestle" was the origin of another Greek word, *Palaestra*. Formed from the word *pale*, the word *Palaestra* means *to fight* or *to struggle* and depicts *combat*. It describes a house of combat sports, similar to a modern-day gym but on steroids!

'Anything Goes' Wrestling Matches

In the ancient Greek and Roman world, every major city had a gym and a Palaestra. Regular sportsmen would go to the gym, but only the most serious contenders would go to the Palaestra. The average person would never go to the Palaestra to fight because it was the place where the fiercest combatants fought.

In Paul's day, there were primarily three types of sports that took place in the Palaestra. The first was wrestling, which was the most well-known in the Greek world. This kind of wrestling wasn't simply slinging other men to the mat. No, this was such fierce wrestling that some wrestlers actually died. In fact, there were only a few rules to the game — almost anything was allowed. You could use your thumb to gouge out your opponent's eye. You could break his back. You could even break his ribs! Wrestling in the Palaestra was not a joke and could be deadly.

Deadly Boxing Matches — With Knives!

The second sport that took place in the Palaestra was boxing. Boxing in Paul's day was also different than it is today. Boxers today wear boxing gloves, but they are nothing like the gloves boxers wore in the ancient world. To prepare for boxing matches in the Palaestra, boxers took strips of leather that were 16 feet long and would wrap those strips from the elbow all the way around their lower arm again and again until it went across their wrist, across their hand, and finally, across their knuckles. Then a little nail was affixed on each knuckle that was serrated like a small knife so that, when they fought, they would literally draw blood.

Ancient vases of the Greeks often depicted boxers with blood pouring down their face. Some are depicted with a missing ear or nose because they were fighting an opponent with small knives on the end of every knuckle! Just like wrestling, this was a really deadly sport.

Because they were so aggressive and so committed, boxers inside the Palaestra had a rule between themselves that they would not alert their enemy if they had been wounded. There is even an example from the First Century, at the time when Paul was writing Ephesians chapter 6, of a boxer who was hit so hard in the mouth that it knocked out all his front teeth. Rather than spitting out his teeth, he chose to swallow them so his opponent wouldn't know how badly he had been hurt. That is the way they boxed in the Palaestra!

Pankration — Fighting to the Death

The third sport was called *pankration*. It is the combination of the Greek words *pan*, meaning *all*, and *kratos*, meaning *power*. The word *pankration* describes individuals who had more might and power than anyone else. The participants of this sport were the men who survived both the wrestling and boxing matches and came to fight the other survivors. There were absolutely no rules to this game. Participants carried clubs spiked with nails and satchels filled with rocks to sling at their opponents. These men fought and fought until often one of them died.

While this is quite graphic, all these ideas and images are actually found in the word "wrestle" in Ephesians 6:12. The sports that took place in the Palaestra were eye-gouging, back-snapping, blood-spilling sports! Only the most serious contenders would enter the Palaestra to fight. These sports were not for weaklings; they were for someone who was committed to fighting to the very end.

Today, if someone said the word "football," they wouldn't need to stop and explain it because most of us have grown up in a culture where football is nearly worshiped. Everyone knows what football is. That is how the Palaestra was in Paul's day. He didn't need to explain it to his readers. They all knew what this word meant. Paul was describing an eye-gouging, back-snapping, blood-spilling event, and by using this word "wrestle" to describe the forces we are contending with, Paul was asking his audience, "Are you serious about winning this battle? Because you will only survive this intense spiritual warfare if you are committed to go all the way to the end." We must be more committed than the enemy himself!

The Commitment of Our Enemy

Many years ago, Rick was frustrated and discouraged by the victories of the enemy. He tells the following story in the program:

> I said to the Lord, 'I don't understand. We pray for people, and they die. It seems like the enemy is just winning victory after victory. The Church is not demonstrating the power that it should

demonstrate. Lord, why does it seem that the devil is winning all the victories?'

The Holy Spirit answered me and said, 'Because the devil has something the Church doesn't have.'

'Well, what could that be?' I asked. 'We've got the blood of Jesus. We've got the power of the Holy Spirit. We've got the promises of the Word of God. We've got spiritual weaponry. We've got everything! What does the devil have that the Church doesn't have?'

Then I heard the Holy Spirit say, 'The devil has *commitment*, *organization*, and *discipline*. That's what the Church does not have.'

Think about it: commitment, organization, and discipline. How true that is! Some people don't even know whether or not they're going to go to church on Sunday! They keep going back and forth, saying, "Maybe we will. Maybe we won't. Maybe we will stay home or maybe we will do something else." When we look at how believers are today, it begs the question, *"Where is the commitment? Where is the discipline? Where is the organization?"* Very often the Church is so disorganized one doesn't even know who is in charge.

Friend, we must change this. We are going against an enemy that has all of these! The devil is committed, the devil is organized, and the devil is disciplined. He does not have the amount of power we have, but he is more dedicated to his cause than most believers are.

We have the power of the Holy Spirit. We have the blood of Jesus. We have spiritual weaponry. We have the promises of God's Word. We have everything we need to defeat the enemy. If we would match the commitment, organization, and discipline found in the devil's kingdom, we would completely defeat him and keep him under our feet! The problem is the Church is lacking in commitment, organization, and discipline. God has given us everything else!

'We Do Not Wrestle With Flesh and Blood'

Coming back to Ephesians 6:12, it says, "For we wrestle...." Again, that word "wrestle" is *pale* and carries within it the idea of *a Palaestra* — where very committed athletes wrestled in an eye-gouging, back-snapping, blood-spilling event. Then the verse goes on to say, "For we wrestle not with flesh and blood...."

What does that mean? If we don't wrestle with flesh and blood, who do we wrestle with? "...But against principalities, against powers, against the rulers of the darkness of this world, against spiritual wickedness in high places" (Ephesians 6:12).

Notice that one word is repeated four times in this verse: 1) *against* principalities, 2) *against* powers, 3) *against* rulers of the darkness of this world, 4) *against* spiritual wickedness in high places. Each time Paul used the word "against," he used the Greek preposition *pros*, which describes *an intimate encounter.*

An example of *pros* is found in John 1:1, describing the relationship between God the Father and the Son. It says, "In the beginning was the Word, and the Word was with God...." The word "with" is *pros*. It describes God the Father and the Son being so close to each other that they can nearly feel each other's breath on the other's face. They are side by side or face to face. In fact, some expositors translate this as, "In the beginning was the Word, and the Word was face to face with God." That is based on this preposition *pros*, which Paul used four times in this one verse to describe how close we can be to these unseen evil forces.

You need to be prepared for this battle because there will be times when you will feel that you're face to face with these forces, when you are rib cage to rib cage with them, when you can nearly feel them breathing down your neck or on your face. This is how close the conflict can become. Spiritual warfare is not just something that happens on the other side of the world. At some point in your life, it will come knocking on your door and you will need to know how to deal with it. It is important to know who the enemy is and how to defeat him so you can keep him under your feet.

The Evil Ranks of Our Enemy

The word "principalities" is the Greek word *archas* which describes something similar to an archbishop — something that is *chief, the principal,* or *the top.* In this verse, we find that these high-ranking demon spirits are strategically placed over all these other dark forces.

Paul also mentioned "powers," which is the Greek word *exousias* and describes *those that have received license to exercise their dark, demonic influence wherever they wish to demonstrate it.*

Next, Paul mentioned "the rulers of the darkness of this world" which is translated from the Greek word *kosmokratoras.* It is the compound of two Greek words, *kosmos*, describing *something that was ordered*, and *kratos*, meaning *power.* When compounded together, it describes *power that has been organized and disciplined.* In the First Century, it was used to describe taking the raw power of young men who had never been disciplined and bringing them together into a boot camp to organize them, harness their power, discipline them, and turn them into a force and then, finally, dispatching them as well-trained soldiers.

Demon spirits have been trained to do what they do. They are not out freely roaming around doing whatever they wish — they've been harnessed, organized, and disciplined before being dispatched.

Ephesians 6:12 also says we fight against "spiritual wickedness in high places." The word "wickedness" is the Greek word *poneros*, which describes *that which is absolutely insidious or malevolent.*

The phrase "high places" describes *the atmosphere where we live* or *the air we breathe.* Once demon spirits have been taught to do what they do, they are dispatched into the environment where human beings live and are ordered to do malevolent things to us. But the great news is that we have been given the spiritual weaponry to stop every attack of the enemy!

We do not violently wrestle with flesh and blood; our battle is with the unseen, dark spiritual forces assaulting our lives daily. If we as the Church can join together and remain committed, disciplined, and organized, the devil and his evil forces won't be able to stand a chance! We've been given all we could ever need to be completely victorious in Christ as long as we're committed to fight to the very end!

In our next lesson, we will dive into what the Bible says about the dark, spiritual forces we're up against — demons — so we can be completely prepared.

STUDY QUESTIONS

Study to shew thyself approved unto God, a workman that needeth
not to be ashamed, rightly dividing the word of truth.
— 2 Timothy 2:15

1. What were the three sports found in the Palaestra? Why were they considered such deadly sports? Why do you think Paul decided to use the Greek word *pale* when talking about wrestling not against flesh and blood, but against dark, spiritual forces (*see* Ephesians 6:12)?

2. What are the three things that the devil has but the Church doesn't? Why do you think the Church is lacking in these three things?

3. Explain the meaning of the Greek word *pros* as found in Ephesians 6:12 and John 1:1. Compare and contrast the use of *pros* in these two verses.

PRACTICAL APPLICATION

But be ye doers of the word, and not hearers only,
deceiving your own selves.
— James 1:22

1. Are you currently in a battle that feels like you will never win? If so, call a trusted friend and ask them to pray for you. Do not allow the enemy to isolate you, especially in the midst of the battle.

2. The devil and his demonic forces are always looking for a way into our lives. We must stand strong together and fight the good fight of faith by being more committed, disciplined, and organized (*see* 1 Timothy 6:12). Pray and ask the Holy Spirit to put someone on your heart who needs a word of encouragement. Determine to call, text, or email the individual He brings to your thoughts and let them know God brought him or her to your heart.

3. Examine your faith walk. Are you as disciplined or committed to the fight of faith as you could be? What are some areas you can work on? Once you pinpoint any weak areas in your life, come up with a few small steps or goals that you can work toward to achieve victory in your life.

TOPIC

What the Bible Teaches About Demons

SCRIPTURES

1. **Ephesians 6:12** — For we wrestle not against flesh and blood, but against principalities, against powers, against the rulers of the darkness of this world, against spiritual wickedness in high places.

2. **Mark 16:17** — And these signs shall follow them that believe; In my name shall they cast out devils; they shall speak with new tongues.

GREEK WORDS

1. "principalities" — ἀρχὰς (*archas*): chief, principal, or top rulers; where we get the word "archbishop"; refers to high-ranking demon spirits who hold the highest seats of power

2. "powers" — ἐξουσίας (*exousias*): those who have received delegated power; often translated "authority"; here it describes a sub-level of demons who have received license to exercise their dark influence wherever they wish to demonstrate it

3. "rulers of the darkness of this world" — κοσμοκράτορας (*kosmokratoras*): a compound of κόσμος (*kosmos*), which describes something that is ordered, and κράτος (*kratos*), meaning power; together, it pictures power that has been highly organized or disciplined; used in the First Century to describe taking the raw power of young men and training them as soldiers — organizing them, disciplining them, and harnessing that raw power into a powerful force that is then dispatched

4. "wickedness" — πονηρός (*poneros*): insidious, malevolent, or wicked

5. "high places" — ἐπουρανίοις (*epouraniois*): the atmosphere in which humans live; the air below the mountaintops or the air that we breathe

SYNOPSIS

The Bible gives us a very clear description of the devil and the way he and his demonic ranks work to try to keep us bound and enslaved to the weapons he has formed against us. Demons are not aimlessly floating around, but like a well-trained army, they are trained and then dispatched against humanity. As we learn about the Greek meanings behind each rank of demons, we will become better equipped to stand against every attack. In this lesson, we will explore several characteristics of demons found in Scripture.

The emphasis of this lesson:

It is important to know what spiritual forces we are dealing with and understand what the Bible says about them. As we turn to Scripture, we can see that demons have a hierarchy as is described in Ephesians 6:12. Satan's spiritual forces are highly organized and trained for specific tasks. However, they are fearful beings, and they tremble at the name of Jesus. When believers resist them in the authority of Christ, they have no choice but to flee!

The Four Ranks of Evil Spiritual Forces

In the previous lesson of *WEAPONS!*, we focused on Ephesians 6:12 where Paul said, "For we wrestle not against flesh and blood, but against principalities, against powers, against the rulers of the darkness of this world, against spiritual wickedness in high places." In this lesson, we are going to take a deeper look into what each of these four ranks of demonic powers are.

Principalities

In this verse, Paul said our wrestle is "against principalities." The word "principalities" is the Greek word *archas* and describes *those who have the chief seats or chief positions of power.* They are *at the very top.* Satan's kingdom is highly organized, and this word is describing a particular group of ruling spirits at the very top called "principalities."

In the previous lessons of this study guide, we learned some important ways to block the devil's access into our lives. One way the devil often successfully enters our lives is in the area of finances, but God has given us a way to block his access in that area of our life. Rick shares a personal testimony about learning this important lesson in a later program.

Powers

Directly under these principalities are "powers." The Greek word for "powers" is *exousias*. It describes a sublevel of demon spirits that have received the license and authority to do whatever they want to do, wherever they want to do it.

Rulers of the Darkness of This World

Another category of demons mentioned in Ephesians 6:12 are "the rulers of the darkness of this world." The Greek word for this phrase is *kosmokratoras*. This word in Greek is quite unique. In fact, Rick recalls the following story in the program regarding his study of this very word:

> I first studied this word when I was a student in university. When I first saw this word, I was perplexed by it because the word *kosmos* describes *something that is highly arranged, ordered, or disciplined.* The second part of the word is *kratos*, which is *power.* When the two words are compounded, *kosmokratoras* describes *raw power that has been harnessed, organized, and disciplined.* This very term was used to describe a boot camp where soldiers were trained and where young men who were not connected were suddenly harnessed together. All that raw power was organized, disciplined, and became a force that was dispatched. In that boot camp, those men were trained to do everything they will do as soldiers in battle.
>
> I remember asking my Greek professor to explain what this word, *kosmokratoras*, had to do with demon spirits. He couldn't give me an answer, so I just shelved it and said to myself, 'Well, one day I'll understand this word.'
>
> Many, many years later, Denise and I were ministering in a little city in a small church, but it was packed out! People were there to receive the Word. One evening we decided to pray for the sick and people came forward.
>
> One man came forward with his wife, and the man had his hands behind his back. As I prayed for him, I said, 'Tell me, how can I

pray for you?' Suddenly, he pulled his hands out from behind his back. His hands were so twisted and gnarled. His fingers were displaced. His fingers were growing into his hand. His thumb was coming out at the wrong place. Both of his hands were just so gnarled and twisted.

I asked him, 'What happened to your hands?'

He was an unbeliever, so he didn't know spiritual language. He hadn't borrowed jargon from any church. He was just speaking from his experience as he said, 'You know, everything was fine, until one day, it was like something came on my hands. I began to have pain in my hands, and my hands began to twist. Over a period of time, they ended up like this. You know, the amazing thing is once my hands were totally destroyed, I felt whatever was on my hands lift and leave — and it left me like this.'

Standing next to him was his wife who had her hands in her pockets. She had also come forward for prayer, so I asked her, 'Why did you come forward for prayer?'

She pulled her hands out and they looked just like her husband's hands. She said, 'He didn't tell you the other part of the story. When that thing lifted off him, it came on me and did the same thing to me.'

Both of them were standing there with hands gnarled, twisted, and deformed.

Instantly, I saw that this was a spirit of affliction that had come on the man, and after it totally ruined his hands, it lifted and came on his wife. When it finished with her, I'm sure it lifted and moved on to someone else, and someone else, and someone else! In that moment my mind went back to this word *kosmokratoras*, a place where soldiers were trained in a boot camp with certain weapons of war. They were taught to do something specific, and then they were dispatched.

It became so clear to me that demon spirits do not do whatever they do by accident. They were trained to do what they do. There are demons of affliction and that is all they do — afflict people. There are demons of cancer, and that is all they do. There are demons of addiction, and that is all they do. There are demons of perversion, and that is their weapon — their tool. When they are finished bringing havoc into one person's life, they dislodge and move on to do it to the next person, and the next, and the next! These evil spirits are trained to do what they do.

Spiritual Wickedness in High Places

The last term in Ephesians 6:12 is "spiritual wickedness in high places." The word "wickedness" is the Greek word *poneros*, which describes *that which is insidious, wicked, or malevolent*. This verse tells us that these wicked forces are dispatched into the air or "high places." The words "high places" come from a Greek word that describes *the air below the mountaintops* or *the air we breathe*. This is describing demonic forces being dispatched into our atmosphere and environment.

In the early 90's, there was a lot of nonsense being taught about demons being way out in the stratosphere and about renting planes to fly up into the heavens to do spiritual warfare. That is complete nonsense.

Once demon spirits are trained, they are dispatched into the air below the mountains — literally the air we breathe. They come down low where people are because their assignment is to kill, to steal, and to destroy. Their purpose is to come into this atmosphere where they can negatively affect people.

Demons As Described in the New Testament

So that we're not confused by the topic of demons, we are going to turn to the Bible and learn what it tells us about demons.

1. Demons are highly organized under Satan's authority.

The first thing we know about demons is that they are highly organized under Satan's authority. We see this in Ephesians 6:12, which we went over in the text above. They are not floating through the air in a disorganized fashion. They have purposes and goals and ranks to keep them focused on their task.

2. Demons have the ability to demonize people.

The words "demon possession" appear in many modern translations of Scripture, but the Greek does not say that. The Greek says people were "demonized." There are very few people that are actually demon-possessed. Most people are demonized. Demons can be driven out of a demon-possessed person or a demonized person. Scripture explicitly teaches that we have authority to cast them out. Rick has cast out many demons, but the truth is that even if a person is set free from a demon, if they are not saved, the demons that were cast out of him or her will return and bring seven more demons with them. The person's latter condition can be worse than it was in the beginning. Jesus taught this in Matthew 12:43-45.

> **When the unclean spirit is gone out of a man, he walketh through dry places, seeking rest, and findeth none. Then he saith, I will return into my house from whence I came out; and when he is come, he findeth it empty, swept, and garnished. Then goeth he, and taketh with himself seven other spirits more wicked than himself, and they enter in and dwell there: and the last state of that man is worse than the first. Even so shall it be also unto this wicked generation.**

3. Demons are seducing in nature and lead people into error.

Demons will always attempt to morally lead people off track for this is one of their specialties. We read about this in First Timothy 4:1:

> **Now the Spirit speaketh expressly, that in the latter times some shall depart from the faith, giving heed to seducing spirits, and doctrines of devils.**

4. Demons frequent places where paganism, idol worship, occult activity, and immorality occur.

Demons thrive in these types of places. The apostle Paul described this explicitly in First Corinthians 10. This is the reason he warned people to stay away from such places.

> **But I say, that the things which the Gentiles sacrifice, they sacrifice to devils, and not to God: and I would not that ye should have fellowship with devils.**
> **— 1 Corinthians 10:20,21**

5. Demons can inhabit animals.

Demons are searching for something to dwell in and if they can't find a person, they will settle for inhabiting an animal. We can see this in several passages throughout the gospels.

> So the devils besought him, saying, If thou cast us out, suffer us to go away into the herd of swine.
> — Matthew 8:31

> Now there was there nigh unto the mountains a great herd of swine feeding. And all the devils besought him, saying, Send us into the swine, that we may enter into them. And forthwith Jesus gave them leave. And the unclean spirits went out, and entered into the swine: and the herd ran violently down a steep place into the sea, (they were about two thousand;) and were choked in the sea.
> — Mark 5:11-13

> And there was there an herd of many swine feeding on the mountain: and they besought him that he would suffer them to enter into them. And he suffered them. Then went the devils out of the man, and entered into the swine: and the herd ran violently down a steep place into the lake, and were choked.
> — Luke 8:32,33

6. Demons will torture people during the Great Tribulation.

The Bible teaches this in Revelation 9:1-7.

> And the fifth angel sounded, and I saw a star fall from heaven unto the earth: and to him was given the key of the bottomless pit. And he opened the bottomless pit; and there arose a smoke out of the pit, as the smoke of a great furnace; and the sun and the air were darkened by reason of the smoke of the pit. And there came out of the smoke locusts upon the earth: and unto them was given power, as the scorpions of the earth have power. And it was commanded them that they should not hurt the grass of the earth, neither any green thing, neither any tree; but only those men which have not the seal of God in their foreheads. And to them it was given that they should not kill them, but that they should be tormented five months: and their

torment was as the torment of a scorpion, when he striketh a man. And in those days shall men seek death, and shall not find it; and shall desire to die, and death shall flee from them. And the shapes of the locusts were like unto horses prepared unto battle; and on their heads were as it were crowns like gold, and their faces were as the faces of men.

7. Demons will be eternally incarcerated by God in a prison called the Abyss.

Demons will be tormented day and night along with the devil, the beast, and the false prophet. And the devil that deceived them was cast into the lake of fire and brimstone, where the beast and the false prophet are, and shall be tormented day and night for ever and ever.

— Revelation 20:10

How Do Demons Behave?

What else does the New Testament teach us about demons? How do they behave? Let's explore some verses that describe what demons are like and how they act.

1. Demons are fearful beings.
(*See* James 2:19.)

In Scripture, demons are noted for screaming and demonstrating that they are fearful beings. Demons don't just bring fear, they are fearful. They are especially terrified of the name of Jesus or of those walking in the authority they have in Jesus.

2. Demons cry out.
(*See* Matthew 8:29.)

The words "cry out" are used in the gospels repeatedly. It is a word that describes an endless, blood-curdling scream. When demons encounter the power of Jesus, they let out a blood-curdling scream because they are terrified of Jesus and the authority of His name.

3. Demons can be panicked or spooked.
(*See* James 2:19.)

James says the demons "tremble" because they can be so spooked and panicked that they literally shake and tremble.

When Rick was a boy and attended a Baptist church, one of his favorite things to do was to run out of the auditorium when the church service was over and jump into the front seat of his dad's car, which was normally parked by the side entrance of the church where a lot of people came out. He would sit in the driver's seat and hover really low just below the steering wheel. Then he would wait for a woman to walk in front of the car, and just when she turned to walk in front of the car, Rick would lay on the horn to spook and scare her. The women he scared would jump and say, "Ricky Renner, why do you do that to us?"

That is what happens when we say the name of Jesus to demon spirits. It panics them. It spooks them.

4. Demons talk and converse.
(*See* Acts 19:15.)

Demons love to talk. In fact, demons talk so much that many times Jesus had to command them to be silent and shut up. Demons talk and talk and talk.

One time, Rick was in a counseling session and the person he was counseling was going on and on. Eventually, Rick realized that this was a demon speaking to him, and he finally told that thing to shut up! He took authority over it and that person was set free!

5. Demons have intelligence.
(*See* Mark 5:7 and Acts 19:15.)

Demons love to talk and communicate, and they have intelligence. They also know things about people. When the demoniac described in Mark 5 saw Jesus heading his way, he began screaming as he recognized that the power Jesus walked in was interfering with the power controlling him. In Acts 19, a demon recognized both Jesus and Paul, demonstrating that it had intelligence.

6. Demons are unclean.
(*See* Mark 1:23,26; 3:30; 5:2,8; and 7:25.)

There are so many scriptures that describe unclean spirits. Jesus often called demons "unclean," and that word describes *something filthy, foul, dirty, and lewd.* Every time Jesus referred to a spirit as being an unclean spirit, it was such an insult. It was the equivalent of saying, "You dirty, stinking, filthy thing." That is also why demons are even willing to live in pigs. They are just dirty, filthy, stinking, unclean spirits.

7. Demons can be violent.
(*See* Matthew 8:28; and Mark 5:3-5.)

If no one takes authority over demons to restrict their activities, they can be violent.

8. Demons can cause terror.
(*See* Matthew 8:28.)

Demons tend to cause terror. In Matthew 8, two men are described. These two demon-possessed men were so scary to people that those passing by would avoid walking anywhere near these two men. Even though demons are themselves fearful beings, they love to bring terror to humans.

9. Demons can demonstrate physical strength.
(*See* Mark 5:4, Luke 8:29, Acts 19:16.)

Until someone takes authority over demonic spirits, they are able to demonstrate physical strength beyond human strength.

10. Demons can cause physical impairments.
(*See* Matthew 9:33, Mark 3:20-27, and Luke 11:14-23.)

In the gospels, we read that there were people who were afflicted with deafness and others who could not speak, and Jesus identified that demon spirits had caused their impairments.

11. Demons can cause suicidal tendencies.
(*See* Mark 5:5 and 9:22.)

In Mark 5, a demon caused a man to cut himself with sharp stones, and in Mark 9, a demon kept throwing a little boy into a fire. This demonstrates that demons can cause humans to have suicidal tendencies.

12. Demons operate through occult activities.
(*See* Matthew 17:15.)

Demons operate through occult activities, we see an example of this in Matthew 17. The Bible describes a little boy as "lunatic." The word "lunatic" means he was *moon-struck*, indicating that his parents were involved with the occult and likely in occult practices that took place during the time of a full moon. While they were involved in occult worship, their son became moon-struck because of their occult activities.

13. Demons can act religious and pray.
(*See* Mark 5:1-17 and James 2:19.)

Demons can also pray, and this is demonstrated in Mark 5 when several demons begged Jesus to send them into nearby pigs rather than empty spaces. So we see that demons can pray and act very religious, but did you know demons can also believe? James 2:19 states that demons believe there is one God.

14. Demons recognize authority.
(*See* Mark 1, Luke 4, and Acts 19.)

When we operate in the authority of Jesus Christ, demon spirits recognize the authority of His name and respond.

15. Demons can be resisted.
(*See* James 4:7.)

James 4:7 says when we resist the devil and demonic powers, they must flee.

16. Demons submit to the name and authority of Jesus.
(*See* Mark 1:27, Luke 4:36, and Acts 19:15.)

The four gospels and the book of Acts are loaded with demonstrations of demons submitting when a believer uses the authority of the name of Jesus.

My friend, it is very important that you know what the Bible says about demons. Mark 16:17 says we are to cast out demons, but we need to know who we are dealing with so we're fully prepared — just as we have seen in Ephesians 6:12, where all these evil forces are described.

> **For we wrestle not against flesh and blood, but against princi-palities, against powers, against the rulers of the darkness of this world, against spiritual wickedness in high places.**

Now that we took the time to dive into the Word of God and see what it says about demons, we can know exactly what we're up against! In the next lesson, we will take a closer look at one example of spiritual warfare in Rick's life.

STUDY QUESTIONS

> Study to shew thyself approved unto God, a workman that needeth
> not to be ashamed, rightly dividing the word of truth.
> — 2 Timothy 2:15

1. Based on the Greek definitions given in this lesson, briefly describe:

   a. principalities (*archas*).

   b. powers (*exousias*).

   c. the rulers of the darkness of this world (*kosmokratoras*).

   d. spiritual wickedness in high places (*poneros*).

2. Why is it important to understand how the demonic realm operates? Did you learn anything new about the demonic realm in this lesson?

3. Study the following verses listed and explain how demonic forces must bow to the authority of Jesus Christ.

   • Mark 1:27, Luke 4:36, and Acts 19:15.

PRACTICAL APPLICATION

> But be ye doers of the word, and not hearers only,
> deceiving your own selves.
> — James 1:22

1. Are you as committed to the Word of God, attending a Bible-believing church, and prayer as the devil is committed to seeking whom he may devour? If you have become lax in any of these areas, make a renewed commitment to be faithful in each of them.

2. Have you ever experienced an identifiable demonic attack in your life? Which piece of the armor of God did you employ to come through your battle victorious?

TOPIC

An Example of Spiritual Warfare

SCRIPTURES

1. **Ephesians 6:12** — For we wrestle not against flesh and blood, but against principalities, against powers, against the rulers of the darkness of this world, against spiritual wickedness in high places.

2. **Mark 4:36** — And when they had sent away the multitude, they took him even as he was in the ship. And there were also with him other little ships.

3. **Mark 4:37** — And there arose a great storm of wind, and the waves beat into the ship, so that it was now full.

4. **Mark 4:38** — And he was in the hinder part of the ship, asleep on a pillow: and they awake him, and say unto him, Master, carest thou not that we perish?

5. **Mark 4:39** — And he arose, and rebuked the wind, and said unto the sea, Peace, be still. And the wind ceased, and there was a great calm.

6. **Mark 4:40,41** — And he said unto them, Why are ye so fearful? how is it that ye have no faith? And they feared exceedingly, and said one to another, What manner of man is this, that even the wind and the sea obey him?

GREEK WORDS

1. "not" — **οὐκ** (*ouk*): emphatically not; the strongest and most emphatic form of "no"

2. "there arose" **γίνομαι** (*ginomai*): something that comes to pass; something that takes you off guard or by surprise; something you did not anticipate

3. "wind" — **ἄνεμος** (*anemos*): gusts of wind; storm-like forces; turbulence

4. "waves" — **κύματα** (*kumata*): one wave after another; wave after wave after wave

5. "beat into" — ἐπιβάλλω (*epiballo*): a compound of ἐπί (*epi*) and βάλλω (*ballo*); ἐπί (*epi*) means over, and βάλλω (*ballo*) means to throw; compounded it means to pick up and throw; to throw over; to throw against; to cast over

SYNOPSIS

Paul told us in Ephesians 6:12 that we are not wrestling against flesh and blood, or only what we can see in the natural realm. There are invisible forces that we can't see with our eyes at work behind the scenes, stealing, killing, and bringing destruction.

But Jesus is our perfect example of how to respond to any attack of the enemy. In one passage we'll look at today, we will see that while the disciples had their eyes fixed on waves caused by a sudden storm that caught them by surprise, Jesus was sound asleep. It wasn't until He was roughly awakened that Jesus dealt with the storm trying to sink their boat. But what He addressed first wasn't the waves like the disciples might have expected. It was the unseen wind.

If there have been persistent problems in your finances, health, or relationships, and you have done everything you know to do in the natural, you might need to — with the guidance of the Holy Spirit — address the unseen realm to bring breakthrough in your situation. Speak to the wind in your life and declare, "Shhhhhh! Peace be still!"

The emphasis of this lesson:

When you are facing unexpected storms and it looks like you are going under, remember what Paul wrote in Ephesians 6:12, "For we wrestle not against flesh and blood...." There are malevolent forces working behind the scenes, but you have the weaponry to overcome them. You are equipped by the power of God's Word and the Holy Spirit inside you.

A Sinister Force Behind the Scenes

In the last few lessons, we've been delving into Ephesians 6:12, where Paul said, "For we wrestle not against flesh and blood...." Our battle, our struggle, our contending, is not with flesh and blood but against dark forces in the unseen realm. Working behind the scenes in the invisible realm are principalities, powers, rulers of the darkness of this world, and spiritual wickedness in high places, and these malevolent forces have been marshaled against us for our destruction. Their motto is to kill, steal, and destroy, but we can take authority over these forces and keep them under our feet.

Notice how Paul began Ephesians 6:12 by saying, "we wrestle not." The word "not" in the Greek language means *very emphatically, absolutely, categorically not* against flesh and blood. If we are honest, how many times do we actually wrestle with flesh and blood with no results?

For example, maybe you are having a financial problem, so you work and work on that problem. You do everything you can, but it seems the problem can't be resolved. Nothing you do seems to be working. If that's the case, there may be something working behind the scenes.

Or perhaps you have a health issue. You go to the doctor, and he gives you medication after medication. You do everything you are being told to do, but the situation never changes. You're only dealing with the flesh and blood symptoms you can see, but there could be something working behind the scenes that is the source of your health issue.

Or maybe you have a relational conflict that feels like it never ends. You keep trying to work it out but it seems as if the more you try to work it out, the worse it gets and the deeper the conflict becomes. It's good you are doing everything you can to work things out, but if nothing is working, there might be a sinister force behind the scenes that is the real cause of this problem.

If there is a sinister force — an invisible force that you're dealing with behind the scenes — it doesn't matter what you do to try to fix your finances or your health or a relationship. If there is an invisible force causing the problem, all you're doing is putting band-aids on the situation. As an example, Rick shared a story in the program about how he learned this very lesson!

> Many years ago, Denise and I believed it was time to print *Life in the Combat Zone*, the book we now give to our new partners. At the time, I knew this book was really going to impact people's lives, but it was going to take a lot of money to get it into print. At that particular moment, everything was going really well in the ministry. It was the younger years of our ministry when we were traveling and preaching in the U.S., and God was building a partner base for us, which was helping us financially. As it

was time to print this book and begin sharing it with people all over the country, suddenly, our finances dried up. It was like our partners met together in some secret convention and decided they would no longer support us.

That didn't happen, but that is what it felt like. The mail stopped coming, contributions halted, and we even had scheduled meetings canceled. I had never had meetings cancel before, and our finances were drying up.

Not only did we not have money to pay the bills, I did not have the money to pay for the printing of *Life in the Combat Zone*. Suddenly, I was thrust into the combat zone just as I was getting ready to publish *Life In the Combat Zone*.

I said to Denise, 'I just don't understand what's happening with our finances. We haven't done anything wrong. We're giving. We've done what the Lord has told us to do. We're about to print this new book that's going to change people's lives. I just don't understand.'

I began to fret and worry. Every day I would pull out the calculator — that was back in the days of calculators — and I would get all of our bills and compare them to the little money we had. I would begin punching in all those numbers and hit the total button to see the outcome. Every single time I hit total, we were in the red! I was wrangling with the calculator, wrangling with the bills, trying to figure out how I could juggle this and juggle that. Every day I found myself obsessed with financial need. I would pray and say, 'God, we need money. God, we need money, money, money!'

Some people say that all rich people think about is their money, but I think poor people think about money more than rich people do. The rich don't worry that they're not going to have money to pay the bills. They just think about where to invest it. But when you don't have money, you constantly think about money. You can become a slave to it. *Where can I get money? Where can I get money?* I found myself nearly a slave to a lack of money.

Every time I prayed, I would cry, 'Money, money, money.' In fact, you would have thought that was God's name because I said 'money' so often. We were really in a tight place. Maybe you've been in a place like that.

One day when I was crying out, the Holy Spirit spoke to me and said, 'You do not have a money problem.'

I said, 'Really? What kind of problem do I have?'

And He said again, 'You don't have a money problem.'

This kind of irked me, so I responded, 'Then please tell me what kind of problem I *do* have.'

Then a third time the Holy Spirit said, 'It is not a money problem.'

Again, I said, 'Please then, tell me what kind of a problem I have.' The Holy Spirit led me to Mark 4, and wow, did I learn something important!

The Realm of the Invisible

Mark 4 recounts the story of Jesus when He and the disciples were getting ready to cross to the other side of the Sea of Galilee. The Bible tells us in Mark 4:36,37: "And when they had sent away the multitude, they took him even as he was in the ship. And there were also with him other little ships. And there arose…"

The words "there arose" are a form of the Greek word *ginomai*, which describes *something that comes to pass*, *something that takes you off guard or by surprise*, or *something you did not anticipate*.

With this idea in mind, the beginning of this verse could be translated, "And taking them completely off guard." The disciples did not anticipate and would never have expected such a huge windstorm — for, out of nowhere, there arose "a great storm of wind." The Greek word for the phrase "great storm of wind" describes *turbulence*. You can't see turbulence, but you can feel the effects of it!

Verse 37 continues on to say, "And there arose a great storm of wind, and the waves beat into the ship, so that it was now full." The word "waves" in this verse describes *a succession of waves*, one wave after another wave. So wave after wave were beating into the ship. The words "beat into" in verse 37 are a form of the Greek word *epiballo*. The word *epi* means *over*, and the word *ballo* means *to throw*. The waves were literally being hurled into the ship.

But the word *epiballo* doesn't really describe what nature does — it describes what a personality does. There was an invisible personality at work. That invisible personality was picking up waves of the sea and throwing them against the ship. One wave after another wave until the ship was full.

If we had been there that night, what do you imagine the disciples would be doing? These were giant, monster, killer waves crashing against the boat one wave after another. There is no doubt the disciples were fighting the waves and bailing out water — all their focus trained on those waves!

Prior to following Jesus, most of these men had been fishermen, and they knew that lake and its weather patterns. If they had sensed the weather was not normal, they would never have taken that boat out on the sea. That is the reason the Greek word *ginomai* is so important. This storm took the disciples completely off guard and by surprise. When they started their trip that evening, it had to have been a great night for sailing. Then, suddenly, this massive succession of waves began hitting that boat as if someone was picking up those waves and hurling them against the boat, and with each wave the boat began filling up until it was almost completely full.

The disciples' entire focus were on those waves. With all their might, they wrangled with those waves, bailing water and fighting for their lives!

Finally, one of them said, "Hey, I think we need Jesus."

Isn't that amazing? How often do we let something in our lives go for a long time trying to deal with it by ourselves until finally we come to our senses and admit, "I think I need to bring Jesus into this situation."

So one of the disciples finally went to inform Jesus about the situation, and verse 38 says, "And he was in the hinder part of the ship, asleep on a pillow."

The word "pillow" describes a small pillow that fit into the very bow of the ship. It was a small triangular-shaped pillow, which means Jesus was laying on that little pillow almost in a fetal position. He was all cuddled up on that pillow in the bow of the ship, sleeping soundly. He was not worried at all. The same storm that sent the disciples into great fear, rocked Jesus to sleep! He slept in the peace of God in the middle of the storm.

Moving to the next verse, Mark 4:38 says, "And he was in the hinder part of the ship, asleep on a pillow: and they awake him, and say unto him, Master, carest thou not that we perish?" The word "awake" in Greek is often translated as the word "resurrection." This means the disciples did not gently wake Jesus; they didn't just nudge Him a little and say, "Jesus, Jesus — we don't mean to disturb you, but we need your help." No, they jerked Him off that couch like it was a resurrection while simultaneously screaming, "Master, carest thou not that we perish?" or "Lord, don't you care? Do you not see? Do you not understand? These killer waves are swamping us! We are going down and the boat is filling up! The waves, the waves, the waves!"

Then in verse 39, it reads, "And he [Jesus] arose, and he rebuked the wind, and said unto the sea, Peace, be still…." The disciples had been fighting the waves, but Jesus stood up and completely ignored the waves. Instead, He lifted His head, looked to the sky, and began to address the wind. Jesus understood the problem was not a wave problem, it was a wind problem. It was an invisible force working behind the scenes.

Before He ever spoke to the waves, Jesus dealt first with the unseen realm and took authority over the wind. Then He simply said to the waves, "Peace be still." He didn't scream at the waves. Instead, it carries the idea that Jesus said to the waves, "Shhhhhhh."

Verse 39 continues, saying, "And the wind ceased, and there was a great calm."

Finally, Mark 4:40 and 41 says, "And he said unto them, Why are ye so fearful? how is it that ye have no faith? And they feared exceedingly, and said one to another, What manner of man is this, that even the wind and the sea obey him?"

Now, notice the order. First Jesus spoke to the wind and then to the sea, and both the wind and sea fell in line. They obeyed Him. Rick continues his story about his financial issue below:

> This is where the Lord led me when I was fighting finances, wrangling with my calculator, and crying, 'Money, money, money.

We lack money! Where is the money? How are we going to pay the bills?'

And the Lord responded, 'You don't have a money problem,' and then led me to this text. Suddenly, I truly understood what God meant when saying that we didn't have a money problem.

Our problem was like the wind. There was an invisible force that had come to attack us because we were making progress and were about to print *Life in the Combat Zone* — a book that was going to change people's lives. The devil wanted to put all of it on hold and that was the reason we had come under this assault. It was not a money problem. It had nothing to do with money or with our partners or with meetings. It was an invisible force working behind the scene.

So Denise and I came together and put all of our bills on the table. Then I said, 'Denise, this is not our problem. Our problem is in the unseen realm.'

Then we lifted our voices just like Jesus did and dealt with the invisible realm. We rebuked it, commanded it to cease and desist, and then we spoke to the finances. And I said, 'Shhhhhh, peace be still.'

Within days, it was like somebody turned the valve back on. The finances began to flow; everything began to flow once again in such a short matter of time. Everything was back in order. The book was printed, nothing was interrupted, and we never had another financial problem. It had been an invisible problem, and I understood that sometimes our battle really isn't with flesh and blood.

If you're experiencing a similar situation to Rick and you are doing everything you can to fix your finances but nothing is working... Or you're doing everything medically you can do to fix your body, and you're still struggling with the same pain, sickness, or disease as before... Or you're doing everything you can do to fix a relationship in your life, but nothing is improving, then maybe you need to look behind the scenes into the invisible realm to see if there is another force coming against you.

This is the reason Paul told us in Ephesians 6:12, "For we wrestle not against flesh and blood, but against principalities, against powers, against the rulers of the darkness of this world, against spiritual wickedness in high places."

Friend, we need to understand there really are malevolent forces at work behind the scenes in society, in politics, in the economy, and in every sphere of influence surrounding us. That is the reason it isn't enough to just deal with politics or only deal with economics or just take practical steps. Of course, you can do all of that, but along with it, you need to lift your voice like Jesus did and address what is working behind the scenes.

STUDY QUESTIONS

**Study to shew thyself approved unto God, a workman that needeth
not to be ashamed, rightly dividing the word of truth.
— 2 Timothy 2:15**

1. Read Second Kings 6:15-17 and compare the similarities between this story and the story in Mark 4:36-41. Why do you think Jesus was sleeping so peacefully in that storm?

2. Define the meaning of "waves" in Mark 4 as described in this lesson, and then explain — according to the Greek word *epiballo* — what caused these waves that brought so much fear to the disciples. Do you think the disciples would still have been afraid if they had expected the storm?

3. Did this lesson open up a new perspective for you on the story of Jesus and the disciples on the boat? What stood out most about the insight you received from this lesson? Was there a word or phrase or idea that you hadn't noticed before?

PRACTICAL APPLICATION

**But be ye doers of the word, and not hearers only,
deceiving your own selves.
— James 1:22**

1. Take a moment to identify any area of your life where you have done all you know to do to bring breakthrough, whether it is in the area of finances, health, or relationships. Ask the Holy Spirit to reveal

to you what may be happening behind the scenes that you have not been aware of and to intervene on your behalf. Find some verses on spiritual warfare — either from this study or elsewhere — to stand on as you gear up for battle.

2. In Mark 4:38, in the middle of the storm, the disciples woke Jesus and accused Him of not caring about them. Have you ever had a time when you felt similarly? How did you overcome that lie from the devil, and how did God demonstrate His faithfulness despite your doubt and fear? How can you remind yourself to remain steadfast when storms arise in the future?

3. Many Spirit-filled Christians get so busy in their lives that they forget to pray in tongues. Take about five minutes to simply pray in the Spirit. When you do this, you will be strengthened in your inner man and clothed in the armor God has provided.

LESSON 9

TOPIC

The Whole Armor of God

SCRIPTURES

1. **Ephesians 6:12** — For we wrestle not against flesh and blood, but against principalities, against powers, against the rulers of the darkness of this world, against spiritual wickedness in high places

2. **Ephesians 6:13** — Wherefore take unto you the whole armour of God, that ye may be able to withstand in the evil day, and having done all, to stand

3. **1 Thessalonians 5:8** — But let us, who are of the day, be sober, putting on the breastplate of faith and love; and for an helmet, the hope of salvation

4. **2 Corinthians 6:4-7** — But in all things approving ourselves as the ministers of God, in much patience, in afflictions, in necessities, in distresses, in stripes, in imprisonments, in tumults, in labours, in watchings, in fastings; by pureness, by knowledge, by long suffering, by kindness, by the Holy Ghost, by love unfeigned, by the word of truth,

by the power of God, by the armour of righteousness on the right
hand and on the left

GREEK WORDS

1. "wherefore" — Διὰ τοῦτο (*dia touto*): wherefore; in light of all of this;
   on account of all I've said; in response to all this; consequently

2. "take unto you" — ἀναλάβετε (*analabete*): a compound of ἀνά (*ana*),
   which means to repeat an action over again, and λάβετε (*labete*),
   meaning to actively receive; together, it means to do it like you once
   did; gives the image of the armor of God laying on the floor around
   you as if it had fallen off

3. "whole armour" — πανοπλία (*panoplia*): a compound of πᾶν (*pan*),
   meaning all, and ὅπλον (*hoplon*), which is the Greek word for weaponry; together, it means absolutely all the weaponry God has provided; pictures a soldier fully dressed in his armor from head to toe;
   the full attire and weaponry of a soldier; the following hardware was
   required for a soldier to be fully dressed for battle: the loinbelt, breastplate, shoes, shield, helmet, sword, and lance

SYNOPSIS

On his third missionary journey, Paul encountered believers who had
not yet heard about the baptism in the Holy Spirit. He laid his hands on
them, and they were filled with the Holy Spirit and spoke in tongues.
Amazing miracles took place, and many people turned from occult
practices. Large numbers of people came to know Christ, which resulted
in the formation of the church at Ephesus — making it the largest church
at the time. But despite the church of Ephesus being born out of the
power of the Holy Spirit, not many years later, the Ephesian believers had
backslidden so much that they were grieving the Holy Spirit, and their
spiritual armor had fallen off. Paul encouraged those believers to pick up
their spiritual armor again. He reminded them of the importance and
purpose of each piece of their God-given spiritual armor.

The emphasis of this lesson:

**Each of the seven pieces of armor are vital in spiritual warfare. Being
clothed in God's spiritual armor daily is essential for living a victorious Christian life. As time goes on, we can lose our spiritual fervor,
and the armor of God can fall off us if we don't make it a point to dress**

ourselves with our spiritual armor every single day. God has given us all the weaponry we need to succeed: the loinbelt of truth, the breastplate of righteousness, the shoes of peace, the shield of faith, the helmet of salvation, the sword of the Spirit, and the lance of prayer.

'As a Result of All I Have Told You'

In our previous lessons, we examined the demonic hierarchy of the kingdom of darkness and discovered that demons are highly trained, organized, and dispatched into the realm where humans live. We have also discussed several characteristics of demons as recorded throughout the New Testament.

In the last lesson, we spent time examining Mark 4:36-41, where the disciples and Jesus experienced a violent storm while crossing a lake. It is here we see that Jesus dealt first with the unseen wind before addressing the tall waves. In a similar way, when we're struggling with storms in our finances, health, or relationships, sometimes we can be focused on the wrong issue and not deal with the root of the problem. The problem might not be finances, health, or relationships; the problem might be in the invisible realm. For as Ephesians 6:12 says, "…We wrestle not against flesh and blood, but against principalities, against powers, against the rulers of the darkness of this world, against spiritual wickedness in high places."

In this lesson, we will return to verse 13 of Ephesians 6, which says, "Wherefore take unto you the whole armour of God, that ye may be able to withstand in the evil day, and having done all, to stand."

The Greek word for "wherefore" is *dai touto* and could be better translated as *in light of all this, as a result of all I have told you*, or *consequently*. Paul was basically saying, "In light of the fact that God has given you power for the fight, in light of the fact that there is an enemy who really wants to take you down, and in light of the fact that there are principalities, powers, rulers of the darkness of this world, and spiritual wickedness that have been dispatched into our environment to attack us; in light of all these things, take on the whole armor of God."

The words "take unto you" are from the Greek word *analabete*, which means *to repeat the action*. It is a compound of two words, *ana* and *lambano*. The word *ana* means *to repeat the action* or *to pick something up*, while the word *lambano* means *to take*. When these two words are combined, it means *to repeat what you did previously*, *to pick it up*, or *to receive again*.

At the time Paul was writing this letter to the church of Ephesus, the church was failing on a practical level — despite once being filled with the greatest knowledge and revelation — because they were no longer walking in the power of God. This is astonishing because Acts 19 describes how, at its inception, the church of Ephesus was birthed out of tremendous power. The power of God exploded during Paul's third missionary journey, and more and more people were coming to Christ until the Ephesian church became the largest in the world during the First Century. It also became a missionary-sending church and hosted Christians from around the world to study at the feet of leaders in the city of Ephesus. However, at the time Paul was writing his letter to the church at Ephesus, many had stopped walking in that power of God and in the revelation of His Word.

Problems in the Church at Ephesus

Ephesians 4:25-31 describes problems that existed in the church at Ephesus:

They had a lying problem.

- "Wherefore putting away lying…" (v. 25).

They had an anger problem.

- "Be ye angry and sin not…" (v. 26).

They had an access problem.

- "Neither give place to the devil" (v. 27).

They had a stealing problem.

- "Let him that stole steal no more…" (v. 28).

They had a communication problem.

- "Let no corrupt communication proceed out of your mouth…" (v. 29).

They had a behavior problem.

- "…Grieve not the holy Spirit of God…" (v. 30).

They had an attitude problem.

- "Get rid of all bitterness, wrath, anger, clamour, evil speaking, and malice" (v. 31).

All these horrible behaviors and attitudes were present in the "great" church of Ephesus. Their behavior was so atrocious that they were actually grieving the Holy Spirit. This only shows that we must be serious about our spiritual life. With this example in mind, we can see that a great beginning in our walk with God doesn't guarantee a great ending. Beginning strong by walking in the power of God does not mean we will automatically continue to walk in that power. We must be committed to walk in that power every day.

Picking Up Our Spiritual Weaponry

In Ephesians 6:11, we learned that by walking in the power of God, He will clothe us with His spiritual weaponry from head to toe. But if for some reason we backslide and begin to step away from the power of God, our weapons will begin to fall.

The good news, found in Ephesians 6:13, is that we can pick up the weapons that have fallen and start over again. While verse 13 says, "Wherefore take unto you…," the Greek literally means, "Consequently, as a result of all this, do it again — reach down, pick it up, put it on, and receive it like you once did."

Here Paul was talking about the whole armor of God, and he described it in detail throughout this chapter in Ephesians. However, as we mentioned in a previous lesson, Paul gave his first list of spiritual weaponry in the book of First Thessalonians, his oldest epistle.

In First Thessalonians 5:8, Paul said, "But let us, who are of the day, be sober, putting on the breastplate of faith and love; and for an helmet, the hope of salvation." This is the first time Paul ever wrote about spiritual weaponry. His description seems very elementary, but by the time he wrote Ephesians 6, his description had become quite extensive and very well developed. So what changed?

Over the years, Paul had been chained to many different Roman soldiers, and rather than waste time, he began to examine the helmet on the soldier's head, the breastplate he wore, the shield he carried, his sword, his shoes, his belt, and his lance. Then the Holy Spirit began speaking to Paul about spiritual weaponry. Likewise, there are times when God will speak to us through our environment. As Paul was examining all of those pieces of weaponry, he began to get a revelation about the types of weapons God has given us.

In the book of Second Corinthians, Paul wrote,

> **But in all things approving ourselves as the ministers of God, in much patience, in affliction, in necessities, in distresses, in stripes, in imprisonments, in tumults, in labors, in watchings, and in fastings, by pureness, by knowledge, by long suffering, by kindness, by the Holy Ghost, by love unfeigned, by the word of truth, by the power of God, by the armor of righteousness on the right hand and on the left.**
> **— 2 Corinthians 6:4-7**

In verse seven, we can see that we have armor on our right hand and armor on our left. Isn't it wonderful that God has supplied us with all the weaponry we will ever need to keep the devil under our feet and be victorious?

The Whole Armor of God

Again, Paul said in Ephesians 6:13, "Wherefore take unto you the whole armour of God…." In Greek, the phrase "whole armor" is *panoplia*. The word *pan* means *all*, and the word *hoplon* is the Greek word for *weaponry*. When you put it all together, it is describing the *full armor* or *complete weaponry* provided to us by God. The word *panoplia* used in this verse is the very word used to describe the seven pieces of weaponry utilized by every Greek and Roman soldier. There could have been auxiliary pieces, but every serious soldier had these seven pieces found in the text below.

The Loinbelt

The loinbelt was the soldier's first piece of weaponry, and it covered his loins protecting his reproductive organs. It had a buckle on each side, and — on one buckle hung the shield and on the other hung the sword. The loinbelt was such an important piece of armor because it held all the other pieces of weaponry together. Although it was the least impressive piece, it really was the most important. If a soldier did not have his loinbelt, many other pieces would just fall off him. And this is true for us as well. Ephesians 6 says the loinbelt is the "word of truth," and the Word of God really is the central and most important piece of weaponry given to us by God. Without it, all our other weaponry falls off. That is why it is essential for us to read the Scriptures every day.

The Shoes

Another important part of the armor for Roman soldiers was their shoes. Ephesians 6 calls them "shoes of peace." The first part of the shoes were the greaves. They began at the soldier's knee and extended all the way to the ankle. They covered the Roman soldier's shins and shielded his lower legs as he walked through thorns or rocky places while also protecting his legs from attacks of the enemy.

On the feet were sandals, which were very tightly woven. In fact, they were so tight they were difficult to remove. On the bottoms of those sandals were spikes that were meant to hold the soldier's feet in place while he battled enemy forces. If the soldier used his shoes correctly, he could give a good kick to his adversary and kill him. In a certain sense, these were *killer shoes*. It is amazing that, by the inspiration of the Holy Spirit, Paul called them "shoes of peace."

If we use our spiritual shoes of peace correctly, we will have so much peace in our lives. We can rest knowing our legs and feet are protected from the thorny and rocky places in life, we can hold our ground in the midst of any enemy attack, and we can even deliver a killer blow to our enemy!

The Breastplate

The design of the breastplate changed as time passed, but at the time Paul was writing about the breastplate of righteousness during the First Century, it was made of multiple pieces of metal that were tightly held together. The longer the soldier wore his breastplate, the more dazzling it became. As he moved, those pieces of metal would begin to rub against each other and the breastplate would become increasingly more brilliant.

The purpose of the breastplate was to protect the soldier's vital organs. A piece of the breastplate covered the front, and another piece covered the back of the soldier, protecting him on both sides of his body.

In Ephesians 6, Paul called this piece of weaponry in the armor of God "the breastplate of righteousness." Friend, righteousness really is our breastplate that protects our vital organs, including our heart, and makes us dazzle. The longer we walk in our righteousness, the more brilliant we become. We become a holy terror to the enemy. He can't even see the fight because we are so dazzling! That is what righteousness does and the reason it is called the breastplate of righteousness.

The Shield

Every Roman soldier had a shield, and there were two kinds of shields the Romans carried. One was round and was never used in battle. It was called an "aspis" and was only carried in parades. The second shield was used in battle and was very large. The Greek word that describes *this* shield is the same word used for "door" in the Greek language. This shield was as long as it was wide. When a man joined the Roman army, he would be measured from side to side and from top to bottom. Then a shield would be fabricated just for him to ensure he was covered from head to toe and from side to side. In the armor of God, our shield is our faith.

The exterior of the shield was made from wood, and the interior was made of multiple layers of leather and animal hide. Unless it was anointed with oil every morning, it would become very brittle. So the first thing a Roman soldier did each day was to take a vial of oil in a rag and press the oil into his shield to be sure it always had top-notch anointing and to keep it from becoming brittle and cracking because of arrows shot by his enemies. If the shield became fragile or brittle, those arrows could penetrate it. Roman soldiers knew the importance of anointing their shields with oil daily. Likewise, we must keep our faith in top-notch condition. God has given us enough faith to make sure we are covered from top to bottom and from side to side!

The Helmet

The Roman helmet covered the top of the soldier's head, and it had cheek pieces to protect the sides of the face. There was also a large piece that went across the back of the neck. The purpose of this piece was to protect the soldier's neck from the battle-ax of the enemy. These enemies threw the battle-ax like a boomerang, and they knew how to throw it just right to hit the back of the neck and take a soldier's head off. That is the reason the Roman helmet was designed to protect the top, the sides, and the back of the head — to be sure that soldier would not lose his head!

In Ephesians 6, Paul called our spiritual helmet "the helmet of salvation." This tells us we really need to know in our head what we believe about our salvation. Our minds need to be protected, or the devil will wreak havoc on our lives.

The Sword

In Ephesians 6:17, the sword is called "the sword of the Spirit." The Roman sword was double-edged and usually used for up-close combat. In the same way, we must use the Holy Spirit for face-to-face combat with the enemy.

The Lance

For the Roman soldier's armor to be complete, there was a seventh piece of weaponry he would carry called the lance or spear. Ephesians 6:18 says, "Praying always with all prayer and supplication in the Spirit," telling us that the lance is *the lance of intercession*. When we pray, it sends this offensive weapon out ahead of us to attack and upend any plots of the enemy.

When we put all these pieces of armor together, it describes the full weaponry of a Roman soldier and the entirety of the armor God has provided for us. This is what Paul had in mind in Ephesians 6:13 when he said, "Wherefore take unto you the *whole armour* of God." God has supplied spiritual weaponry to cover us from head to toe and from one side to the other. Equipped with this deadly armor, we have everything we need in Christ to put the enemy on the run and keep him under our feet where he belongs.

STUDY QUESTIONS

Study to shew thyself approved unto God, a workman that needeth not to be ashamed, rightly dividing the word of truth.
— 2 Timothy 2:15

1. Read through Ephesians 6:10-18, then briefly describe each piece of God's spiritual armor and its purpose.
    - Loinbelt
    - Shoes and greaves
    - Breastplate
    - Helmet

- Shield
- Sword
- Lance

2. God has given us all the weaponry we need for victory! Read the following verses as additional sources on the spiritual weaponry we've been given.
   - The Belt — Ephesians 6:14; 2 Timothy 2:15; John 8:32,16:13
   - The Shoes — Ephesians 6:15; John 16:33; Matthew 5:9; John 14:27; Isaiah 26:3
   - The Breastplate — Ephesians 6:14; Isaiah 59:17; 1 Thessalonians 5:8; Matthew 6:33
   - The Helmet — Ephesians 6:17; Isaiah 59:17,12:2; 1 Thessalonians 5:8
   - The Shield — Ephesians 6:16; 1 John 5:4; Romans 10:17; 2 Corinthians 5:7
   - The Sword — Ephesians 6:17; John 14:26; Romans 8:26
   - The Lance — Ephesians 6:18; Philippians 4:6; 1 John 5:14-15; Romans 12:12
   - Victory — 1 John 5:4; Deuteronomy 20:4; 1 Corinthians 15:57; 2 Corinthians 12:9,10; Romans 8:37

PRACTICAL APPLICATION

But be ye doers of the word, and not hearers only,
deceiving your own selves.
—James 1:22

1. Describe a battle in your life you have come through victoriously. How did you utilize the armor of God in your battle to win? Was there any piece of weaponry you neglected that you could use next time?

2. Explain how you have recently utilized the helmet of salvation in your life. What was the result?

3. Have you ever faced a circumstance or time in your life that caused you to lay your spiritual armor down? Perhaps you have found yourself in a situation similar to the church of Ephesus when, over a period

of time, you let it fall away until you were defenseless. What do you think caused this to happen, and what helped you pick up your spiritual weapons again?

TOPIC

The Most Important Piece of Weaponry: The Loinbelt of Truth

SCRIPTURES

1. **Ephesians 6:10-13** — Finally, my brethren, be strong in the Lord, and in the power of his might. Put on the whole armour of God, that ye may be able to stand against the wiles of the devil. For we wrestle not against flesh and blood, but against principalities, against powers, against the rulers of the darkness of this world, against spiritual wickedness in high places. Wherefore take unto you the whole armour of God, that ye may be able to withstand in the evil day, and having done all, to stand.

2. **Ephesians 6:14** — Stand therefore, having your loins girt about with truth, and having on the breastplate of righteousness.

3. **Ephesians 6:17** — And take the helmet of salvation, and the sword of the Spirit, which is the word of God.

4. **Ecclesiastes 8:4** — Where the word of a king is, there is power....

GREEK WORDS

1. "wherefore" — **Διὰ τοῦτο** (*dia touto*): wherefore; in light of all of this; on account of all I've said; in response to all this; consequently

2. "take unto you" — **ἀναλάβετε** (*analabete*): a compound of **ἀνά** (*ana*), which means to repeat an action over again, and **λάβετε** (*labete*), meaning to actively receive; together, it means to do it like you once did; gives the image of the armor of God laying on the floor around you as if it had fallen off

3. "able" — **δύναμαι** (*dunamai*): depicts strength that makes one able, capable, strong, and powerful; has power; has ability

4. "withstand" — ἀντιστῆναι (*antistenai*): to stand against; to push against; to aggressively position oneself against

5. "stand" — στῆναι (*stenai*): to stand; pictures a victorious soldier standing upright and his shoulders thrown back

6. "evil" — πονηρός (*poneros*): malevolent, malicious, sinister, or wicked

7. "stand" — στῆτε (*stete*)to stand upright; pictures one so confident that he stands with his head held high and his shoulders thrown back

8. "word" — ῥῆμα (*rhema*): a fresh, specific spoken word; a suddenly quickened word

SYNOPSIS

The loinbelt of truth, or the Word of God, is the most vital piece of weaponry in our arsenal, and it is the only piece of weaponry that has passed from the unseen, spiritual realm into the physical realm. If God's Word is not a vital and central part of our daily lives with the Lord, we will lose our peace and have a diminished sense of our righteousness in Him. Every piece of weaponry God has made available to us is very important, but the loinbelt of truth is the most essential because it holds all the other pieces of armor together. In the midst of every battle, God has a snapshot of you, and it is not a picture of defeat; it is a picture of glorious victory against the devil and his demonic forces!

The emphasis of this lesson:

The written Word of God must become the highest priority in our life. When God's Word does not have a central place in our walk with the Lord, we will not understand who we are in Christ, and we will be open to every attack of the devil and his demonic forces. While all pieces of God's armor are important, the Word of God holds everything together and is the only visible piece of weaponry in our arsenal.

Put On the Full Armor of God

Previously, we have learned that we are at war with unseen, spiritual forces that are determined to steal from, kill, and destroy anyone who gives them a foothold into their lives. But rather than running from the enemy in terror, God has given us an arsenal of weaponry to win battles and come out victorious!

In the last lesson, we learned about each of the seven pieces of armor described in Ephesians 6. We have also seen that in Ephesians 6:10, Paul described the power we need for fighting spiritual battles and the importance of being filled with the Holy Spirit. In this lesson, we will examine in detail the very first weapon listed in Ephesians 6:14 — the loinbelt of truth.

Before we delve further into the loinbelt of truth, let's do a quick review of what we've learned so far.

Finally, my brethren, be strong in the Lord and in the power of his might. Put on the whole armor of God that ye may be able to stand against the wiles of the devil. For we wrestle not against flesh and blood, but against principalities, against powers, against the rulers of the darkness of this world. And against spiritual wickedness in high places. Wherefore take unto you the whole armor of God that ye may be able to withstand in the evil day, and having done all, to stand.
— Ephesians 6:10-13

"Wherefore" is the Greek phrase *dia touto*. A better translation would be *in light of all of this* or *in response to what I have said*. It basically means, "In light of the fact that God has given you power for the fight; in light of the fact that God has provided you with all the weaponry that you need; in light of the fact that there is a real devil out there whose motto is *to kill, steal, and destroy*; in light of the fact that the devil has organized his forces and has marshaled them against us; in light of all of this, take unto you the whole armor of God."

The words "take unto you" are the Greek word *analabete*, which is a compound of *ana* and *lambano*. The word *ana* means *to repeat the action again*, and it also carries the idea of *something that is coming upward*. The word *lambano* means *to take* or *to receive*. When both words are combined, it means *to repeat the action, to reach down, to pick it up, to raise it up*, or *to put it back on the way you once wore it*. This reveals that the church at Ephesus had dropped their weaponry.

There are times in life when we drop our weapons along the way, and the way we drop our spiritual weaponry is by not walking in the power of God. When we are endued with power by the Holy Spirit, that supernatural power is what equips us with the full armor of God. But the day we cease walking in God's power is the day the weaponry begins to fall off.

This doesn't mean we lose our salvation, but we discard a lot of our weaponry when we're not walking in that divine power. However, when we are refilled with the Holy Spirit and choose to start walking in that power again, it will put a helmet on our head, a breastplate on our chest, a loinbelt around our waist, a shield in our hand, a sword at our side, greaves and shoes on our feet, and a lance on our back.

The power of God will fully outfit us so we are ready to deal with the devil. And we must put on the *whole* armor, which means there are not just one or two pieces of weaponry. We must put on God's whole armor so we can sufficiently stand against the devil.

Going back to verse 13, it says, "Wherefore take unto you the whole armour of God, that ye may be able…." The phrase "that ye may be able" is a form of the Greek word *dunamai* and could be read, "that ye may be sufficiently powerful to withstand."

The Greek word for "withstand" is *antistenai* and is a combination of *anti*, which means *against*, and *histemi*, meaning *to stand against and to push the devil back across the line*. When we are outfitted in all the weaponry God has provided, we are no longer being pursued by the enemy; we are the ones in pursuit. Because of the power of God that has outfitted us in our spiritual weaponry, we are now in a position to stand against and push him back across the line. This means, if he has our health, we can push him out of our health. If the devil is messing with our kids, he no longer has the right to be there. When we are dressed in the whole weaponry of God, we can push him back across the line from any area of our lives: our kids, our marriage, our finances, our relationships — any area the enemy is trying to attack.

'Withstand in the Evil Day, and Having Done All, To Stand'

Continuing on with Ephesians 6:13, it says, "Wherefore take unto you the whole armor of God, that ye may be able to withstand in the evil day…." What is the evil day? The Greek word for "evil" is a form of *poneros* and describes what is *malevolent*, *sinister*, *wicked*, or *malicious*.

Any day you wake up and evil gets into your day, that is an evil day. But evil has no right to be there because you are a child of God. You have been translated out of the kingdom of darkness and into the Kingdom of His dear Son where there is no darkness at all (*see* Colossians 1:13). If darkness is trying to invade your life, it has no right to be there. You have every right to say, "This evil does not belong to me. It should not be a part of my day. I'm pushing this evil back across the line. Evil, you have no right to be in my life!"

Anytime you get a bad report from the doctor, get a flat tire, the refrigerator breaks down, you suddenly receive a bill you didn't know was coming, or discover there is strife in a relationship, every one of those are evil things that just show up in your day and they have no right to be there to steal your day, your joy, your time, or your attention. When you have put on the whole armor of God, you can look at every one of those situations and say, "This malevolence, this malicious thing, this sinister activity has no right to be in my life! I live in the kingdom of light. That darkness does not belong here, and I'm pushing it back across the line because it does not belong in my life!"

Verse 13 continues, "...And having done all, to stand." This section of the verse is somewhat of a misnomer because it *sounds* a little like this: "If you used the weapons of God and they don't work, then just stand. If you used the name of Jesus and it doesn't work, then just stand. If you used your faith and it doesn't work, then just stand. If you've done everything and nothing is working, then just stand."

But friend, this is not accurate. If the weapons don't work, if the name of Jesus doesn't work, if the blood of Jesus does not have power, if the power of the Holy Spirit can't do the job, then what do you think standing is going to do?

Well, this is what the Greek says in verse 13: "And having brought everything to an ultimate conclusion, stand." This is God's snapshot of you at the end of the battle. God is prophesying, and He sees you having brought the battle to a conclusion. You have been through every stage of the struggle. You have fought. You have slugged it out. You have gone step by step all the way to the conclusion. And at the end of the fight, you are not the one lying under the devil's feet; the devil is under *your* feet! God is saying, "Let Me show you this snapshot I have of you. It is a picture of what you look like at the end of the fight!"

You may feel like you're going through a rough time. When you're in the middle of a spiritual conflict, it may feel very difficult, stressful, and discouraging, but God has a photograph of you at the end of your battle.

When you have come through the battle, you will not be lying on the ground in a bloody mess; no, you will be standing upright with your shoulders thrown back, your head held high, a sword raised high in the air with the enemy under your feet. Having brought the battle to an ultimate conclusion, you will be the one standing, not the enemy!

This is a prophetic word for you. Friend, take it by faith. Say, "God has a photo of me and when this thing is done, I'm going to be the one standing with the enemy under my feet! Amen!"

The Most Important Piece of Weaponry — the Loinbelt of Truth

In Ephesians 6:14, Paul continued, "Stand therefore, having your loins girt about with truth, and having on the breastplate of righteousness." The word "stand" means *to stand up straight, hold your head high, and throw your shoulders back*. Roman soldiers didn't walk all hunched over in defeat. They knew they had everything they needed to defeat the enemy, and they stood victoriously and confidently.

When Paul said, "Stand therefore," it means stand up straight, hold your head high, throw your shoulders back, push your chest out, and be proud of who you are. You're dressed in the whole weaponry of God.

Paul then began to describe the weapons God has given us. The first piece of armor Paul described was the loinbelt. Why would Paul begin with the loinbelt? There are so many other pieces of weaponry that were more beautiful and exciting to talk about.

For example, there was the helmet. The Roman helmet was quite outstanding. It had this mane of horsehair on the top, which was usually multicolored — it was so noticeable. There was the long lance and a massive sword, which the Roman soldier carried. Or there was also the dazzling breastplate. These were all outstanding pieces of weaponry. But even though the loinbelt was the most uninteresting, boring piece of weaponry, Paul began describing this piece first because it was the most important piece of all.

The loinbelt covered the loins. It wrapped completely around the soldier's waist and was very central to the Roman soldier's armor. It was so central that if he wasn't wearing his loinbelt, his weaponry would fall to pieces.

If you saw Rick at this moment and were asked to describe what he was wearing, what would you describe first? You'd probably talk about his sweater or shirt, and you might even mention his pants or shoes! But you probably wouldn't say, "Wow! Did you notice Rick's belt? What an amazing belt!" In fact, you probably wouldn't notice his belt at all.

But belts still have a function. Some people, if they don't wear a belt, their pants would fall right off! That is what the Roman soldier's loinbelt did — it kept his other weaponry in place and it also protected the loins.

When he described the armor of God, what spiritual weapon did Paul assign to the loinbelt by the inspiration of the Holy Spirit? He said, "...Having your loins girt about with truth..." (Ephesians 6:14). The word "truth" in this verse refers to *the written Word of God*.

But we also see "the word of God" mentioned in another place within the armor of God. Ephesians 6:17 says, "And take the helmet of salvation, and the sword of the Spirit, which is the *word* of God."

The word "word" in this verse is the Greek word *rhema*. It describes *a fresh, spoken word*, and it acts like a spiritual sword. By comparison, when verse 14 says "having your loins girt about with truth," it is referring to the centrality of God's *written* Word in our lives. The Word of God is so very important, and it is the only weapon we have that has left the invisible realm and passed into the visible, physical realm.

Rick is righteous, but you would not be able to see his breastplate of righteousness. He is saved, but you can't see his helmet of salvation. You can't see his sword of the Spirit or his shield of faith, and if you looked at yourself, you wouldn't see these pieces of spiritual armor on you either because none of them are visible.

Our Only Visible Piece of Weaponry

There is one weapon that is visible and so central to our lives. It holds all the other pieces of the armor together and has actually passed into the natural realm. We can even hold it in our hands. It is the written Word of God. The Bible is the most important piece of weaponry God has passed into our hands. This does not diminish the importance of the other pieces of weaponry God has given us, but if the Bible is not wrapped around us as the most central part of our lives, we will begin to lose our peace, because peace is a byproduct of the Word of God in our lives. If we are not walking in the Word, we will begin to lose our sense of righteousness. When we are rooted in the Word of God, we can walk in an awareness of our righteousness. If we are not rooted in the Word, we will not understand all the benefits of our salvation. The Word of God is central to everything in our life.

Just as the loinbelt was central to a Roman soldier's weaponry, the Word of God must be central to our life. As long as we are walking in the Word, we will not fall to pieces. The Word of God will hold us together. In fact, this is the reason why Rick always quotes Ecclesiastes 8:4, "Where the word of a king is, there is power…," at the end of his programs — because God's Word has power.

It is not the word of man; it is the written Word of God that has power. Peter stated that we are born again by the Word of God (*see* 1 Peter 1:23), which means the Word contains the reproductive ability of God! As long as we are in the Word, we will be able to move in supernatural power to reproduce and create and multiply. But the day we move away from the Word of God, we will lose our ability to reproduce.

That is the reason the loinbelt importantly covered the Roman soldier's loins. The enemy would try to kick the Roman soldier in his loins to affect his ability to reproduce. If we want to become productive and stay productive, we must stay in the Word of God because it contains the reproductive ability of God.

Paul mentioned the loinbelt first in Ephesians 6:14 because it was the most central piece of spiritual weaponry. We must be determined to be in the Word of God every day so that our spiritual weaponry remains top-notch. If you do not know how to read your Bible, please reach out to RENNER Ministries, and we will provide you with a daily Bible reading plan to help you make the Word of God a central foundation in your life to anchor your life and bring stability.

STUDY QUESTIONS

Study to shew thyself approved unto God, a workman that needeth not to be ashamed, rightly dividing the word of truth.
— 2 Timothy 2:15

1. Ephesians 6:13 says that when we put on the whole armor of God, we can "withstand the evil day." Based off what you read in this lesson, what would you say "evil day" means? Did you have a different interpretation of this part of the verse before? Read this verse in various translations and write down the impression each verse gives you.

2. In this lesson, we learned just how essential the loinbelt is to the Roman soldier. Why is this seemingly uninteresting piece of weaponry so valuable? And why do you think Paul associated "truth" with the loinbelt in Ephesians 6:14?

3. Why do you think the Word of God is the only weapon in our spiritual armor that has been brought into the physical realm? Read the following verses as you answer this question:
   - Hebrews 4:12; Matthew 4:4; John 1:1; 2 Timothy 3:16,17; John 17:17
   - Matthew 24:35; Isaiah 40:8; 1 Peter 1:25

PRACTICAL APPLICATION

**But be ye doers of the word, and not hearers only,
deceiving your own selves.
—James 1:22**

1. The Word of God contains the ability to produce. Read Luke 1:26-38. What was the Word Mary received and what did it produce? Have you ever seen God's Word produce something in your life? What happened?

2. Colossians 1:13 says, "Who hath delivered us from the power of darkness, and hath translated us into the kingdom of his dear Son." Because we have been translated into the kingdom of Jesus where there is no darkness, evil has no place in our life — no matter how small it may seem. Look at your life these last few days. Have you taken authority over the seemingly small but evil inconveniences in your life? How will you go about using your God-given authority moving forward?

TOPIC

The Breastplate of Righteousness

SCRIPTURES

1. **Ephesians 6:13** — Wherefore take unto you the whole armour of God, that ye may be able to withstand in the evil day, and having done all, to stand.

2. **Ephesians 6:14** — Stand therefore, having your loins girt about with truth, and having on the breastplate of righteousness.

3. **2 Corinthians 5:21** — For he hath made him to be sin for us, who knew no sin; that we might be made the righteousness of God in him.

4. **Isaiah 59:17** — For he put on righteousness as a breastplate....

GREEK WORDS

1. "withstand" — **ἀντιστῆναι** (*antistenai*): to stand against; to push against; to aggressively position oneself against

2. "evil" — **πονηρός** (*poneros*): malevolent, malicious, sinister, or wicked

3. "stand" — **στῆναι** (*stenai*): to stand; pictures a victorious soldier standing upright

4. "therefore" — **οὖν** (oun): a conjunction; consequently; accordingly; hence; as a result

5. "word" — **ῥῆμα** (*rhema*): a fresh, specific spoken word; a suddenly quickened word

SYNOPSIS

Every believer has been given powerful spiritual weapons that enable us to push back against any evil attack in our life. The moment we are born again, we are clothed in a spiritual breastplate that protects us on all sides, and we become the very righteousness of God in Christ Jesus!

The emphasis of this lesson:

The ancient Roman soldier wore a dazzling breastplate that was not only beautiful in design but also effective in function. He could walk

boldly and confidently in his breastplate, knowing he was protected on all sides and from every angle.

Power To Drive Out the Invader

God has provided spiritual weaponry for every believer to defeat the enemy, and in this series, we have been studying the complete list of weapons that are available. The apostle Paul described each weapon and its purpose in Ephesians 6, and in the previous lesson, we covered the first and most important piece of weaponry: the loin belt of truth.

We also learned that the evil that tries to infiltrate the life of a believer is an invader that does not belong in our life, and we have the power and authority in Christ to push the devil back and deny him access. When we are dressed in the whole armor of God, we can stand against evil and drive out the invader.

Ephesians 6:13 says,

> **Wherefore take unto you the whole armour of God, that ye may be able to withstand in the evil day, and having done all, to stand.**

The word "withstand" in the original Greek text is *antistenai*. This is a compound of two Greek words, *anti* and *stenai*. The word *anti* means *against* and *stenai* means *to stand*. When compounded, these two words mean that we are literally equipped to *stand against*, *push against*, and *drive out* any evil that attempts to enter our life.

The word "evil" is translated from the Greek word *poneros*, which describes anything that is *malevolent, sinister, malicious,* or *wicked*. You do not have to tolerate any evil attack because you have been equipped with the armor of God to push out of your life anything that is malevolent, sinister, malicious, or wicked. You can refuse to give place to evil in your daily life by learning to live in the armor God has provided for you.

Verse 14 continues, "Stand therefore...." The word "stand" is translated from the word *stenai*, which describes *a Roman soldier who is standing with his shoulders thrown back, his head held high, and his chest protruding forward in great confidence.* It pictures a Roman soldier who is not fearful of anything or anybody because he has been trained and is dressed for battle — he is *dressed to kill.*

The word "therefore" is the Greek word *oun* and means *consequently* or *as a result*. The apostle Paul was essentially saying, "Hold your head up, throw your shoulders back, push your chest out, stand upright. You have every reason to be confident. *Stand therefore.*" The armor of God is a divine set of spiritual weapons that have been imparted to every believer so that we can confidently withstand any attack of the enemy.

The Loin Belt of Truth

After Paul's encouragement in Ephesians 6:14 to "stand therefore," he added, "…having your loins girt about with truth." The loin belt was the most central piece of weaponry a Roman soldier possessed. If he was wearing his loin belt, all of his other pieces of weaponry were held together. But if he was not wearing it, his armor would fall to the ground in pieces.

With the loin belt in place, the breastplate (which was made of two main pieces of metal) was held together so it would not flop back and forth while the soldier was running or fighting. The loin belt was so essential that on either side were two clips — one from which to hang the shield, and the other from which to hang the sword. And on the back of the loin belt was a pouch where the soldier held his various spears, which were used for long-range attacks against the enemy. Without the loin belt, the Roman soldier would not have been properly prepared to withstand an enemy assault.

In the previous lesson, we also learned that the loin belt of truth refers to the Word of God — the Bible. And in Ephesians 6:14, Paul made it clear that the *truth* is as central to our spiritual weaponry as the loin belt was to the Roman soldier's physical weaponry. Of all of the weapons described by Paul, the Bible is the only piece of spiritual weaponry that is also physical; we can actually hold it in our hands.

Every weapon in the armor of God is very real; however, all but one are invisible to the natural eye. The breastplate of righteousness cannot be seen with physical eyes; the shoes of peace are not a tangible piece of weaponry; the shield of faith is invisible; the helmet of salvation cannot be held and literally placed on our head; the sword of the Spirit is not a physical sword; and the lance of prayer is not discernable with natural eyesight.

But the Bible — the loin belt of truth — is the one weapon in God's arsenal that we can pick up, open, read, and keep central in our lives. As long as we keep ourselves rooted in the Word of God, we will be held together. With the Word of God at the center of our lives, our sense of our righteousness in Christ will remain in-tact; we will walk in supernatural peace; we will enjoy all the benefits of salvation; and we will always have faith because faith comes by hearing the Word of God (*see* Romans 10:17). Keeping the Bible central to everything we do will ensure that we are always properly prepared to withstand an enemy assault.

The Bible is so essential that every piece of spiritual weaponry we have been given access to is fully dependent on it — including the sword of the Spirit. Ephesians 6:17 says, "...and the sword of the Spirit, which is the word of God." The Greek word for "word" here is *rhema*, and it describes *a fresh word*, *a spoken* word, or *a suddenly quickened word*. But think about it: In order to wield a sword, you must take it out of its sheath — and the sheath hangs on the *loin belt*. Every *rhema* word we will ever receive from God is rooted in the truth of the Bible. As long as the Bible remains the central focus in our lives, it will hold us together in every area of life.

On the other hand, if we neglect or deprioritize the Scriptures, we will begin to lose our confidence, our sense of peace, and our awareness of the righteousness purchased for us on the Cross. Ultimately, without a steady diet of the truth of the Bible, we will tragically begin to lose our faith, because the Word of God is what holds it all together. *We cannot do without the Word of God!*

The Breastplate of Righteousness

In verse 14 of Ephesians 6, Paul listed the next weapon in the armor of God: "...having on the breastplate of righteousness." The ancient Greek breastplate was designed very simply with a triangular shape and matching front and back pieces. Two additional pieces were fixed on either side, ensuring the soldier was fully protected on all sides of his upper body.

Although effective, the Greek breastplate did not allow for much flexibility or movement, so as the years passed and technology advanced, the breastplate was improved upon. The more technologically sophisticated Romans took the original Greek design to the next level and created a more battle-efficient piece of weaponry.

The new and improved Roman breastplate was primarily made of a front and back piece with multiple pieces of brass tightly woven together above the shoulders with large circular pieces of metal that allowed the soldier to move more freely. Similar to the Greek design, this new breastplate also covered the soldier on the sides, and the metal pieces were woven so tightly that they resembled the scales of a fish. Consequently, the breastplate was the most beautiful and heaviest piece of weaponry in the Roman arsenal.

The longer the Roman soldier walked in his breastplate, the more beautiful it became. As the pieces of metal rubbed against each other, they began to add luster to one another. While the soldier began with a breastplate that was already beautiful, the more he walked in it, the more dazzling it became.

In the same way, our righteousness in Christ Jesus is spectacular and causes us to be dazzling as we walk in it. And the longer we walk in the righteousness purchased for us with the precious blood of Christ, the more dazzling we become! When we are covered with a breastplate of righteousness, we understand that we have been made the righteousness of God in Christ Jesus. As a result, we pray more boldly — not because of who we are, but because of who we are *in Christ Jesus*. Jesus paid a high price for us to have access to His righteousness.

For He [God] hath made him [Jesus] to be sin for us, who knew no sin; that we might be made the righteousness of God in him.
— 2 Corinthians 5:21

God has clothed us in His righteousness, so when He looks at us, He doesn't see someone struggling to be righteous; He sees a magnificent, resplendent, glorious, and dazzling child of God because we are dressed in *His* righteousness!

Bold in the Breastplate of Righteousness

The apostle Paul was not the first to describe righteousness as a breastplate. The prophet Isaiah said,

For He put on righteousness as a breastplate.
— Isaiah 59:17

In both the Old and New Testaments, we see that God considers righteousness to be a piece of armor that protects a person on all sides. And when a person knows he is covered from every angle, he begins to operate with a certain level of confidence and boldness.

Therefore, when we are aware of whose righteousness we have been clothed in, we begin to operate with spiritual confidence and boldness that even affects the way we pray. We no longer approach the throne of grace with shallow, negative, insecure, powerless prayers like, "God, I don't know if I'm worthy enough for you to answer me...." No, when we know that we have been made the righteousness of God in Christ Jesus, His righteousness allows us to pray boldly and confidently.

On the program, Rick described the first time he heard a man who understood God's righteousness pray with great confidence. Hearing the boldness with which the man prayed almost offended Rick because Rick had been raised in a particular religious group who were not very confident when they prayed. So when this man prayed, Rick mistook the man's confidence for arrogance. But the man was not arrogant; he simply knew who he was in Christ. He didn't pray based on his own merit; he prayed based on the merit of Christ's righteousness that had been imparted to him by faith. And if you are born again, that same righteousness of God in Christ has been imparted to you too!

Blinding the Enemy

So far, we have covered three main functions of the breastplate of righteousness. We have seen how the Roman breastplate defended a soldier on all sides, was the heaviest and most beautiful piece of weaponry in the soldier's arsenal, and allowed the soldier to operate with boldness and confidence. But there is more the Roman breastplate could do!

The breastplate was also an *offensive* weapon for the soldier. Because the armor was so bright, when the Roman soldier walked into the sunlight, he was so glorious, dazzling, and resplendent that he would blind the eyes of the enemy. Furthermore, when multiple Roman soldiers approached the enemy as a group, they appeared so bright and shining that the enemy was blinded and couldn't even see to fight them. That is precisely what happens when a body of believers understand and walk in righteousness — it blinds the enemy.

The righteousness of God in which we have been clothed puts the enemy on the run, and it is so powerful that the enemy will flee from us in terror because his vision will be too obscured to launch an attack against us.

When we are clothed in the righteousness of God, we are covered on all sides; God sees us as righteous; we are able to operate with confidence; and the enemy is incapacitated. That is how powerful righteousness is!

And that power is available to any person who calls on the name of Jesus. The moment a person prays the prayer of repentance and Jesus becomes Lord of his life, he becomes the righteousness of God in Christ Jesus. God clothes that person in a robe of righteousness, and he is covered from head to toe! Every person who has made Jesus Lord of his life has this incredible weapon that will protect him on all sides and blind the enemy!

We must understand what it means to be made the righteousness of God in Christ. Without that understanding, we will never be able to pray with authority and confidence, because we will consider ourselves unworthy to ask anything of Him. We are not trying to *become* righteous; we *are* righteous. God has imparted to us the breastplate of His righteousness, and we are justified by faith (*see* Romans 5:1).

So stand therefore, with your head held high, your shoulders thrown back, and your chest out in confidence. As a born-again believer, you are dressed in the whole armor of God with a breastplate of righteousness that protects you and gives you a confidence that blinds the enemy and puts him to flight! That is the power of the righteousness of God in Christ Jesus!

STUDY QUESTIONS

Study to shew thyself approved unto God, a workman that needeth not to be ashamed, rightly dividing the word of truth.
— 2 Timothy 2:15

1. Make a list of the invisible weapons in God's arsenal. What is the one visible weapon we have been given access to and what is the significance of this weapon?
2. What caused the breastplate of the ancient Roman soldier to shine and what increased its sheen? What comparison can be made to your spiritual breastplate of righteousness?
3. How did the ancient Roman soldier cause his enemy to be blinded? Explain how the breastplate of righteousness blinds our spiritual enemies.

PRACTICAL APPLICATION

> But be ye doers of the word, and not hearers only,
> deceiving your own selves.
> —James 1:22

1. Read Hebrews 4:16. What does this verse tell you about the attitude God expects you to have in prayer? Consider your own prayer life. Do you exemplify the words of Hebrews 4:16, or have you allowed your own righteousness to dictate how you approach God?

2. Proverbs 21:31 (*ESV*) says, "The horse is made ready for the day of battle, but the victory belongs to the Lord." Think of a situation in your life that needs God's intervention. How does your new understanding of righteousness impact your faith to push back the enemy?

LESSON 12

TOPIC

The Shoes of Peace

SCRIPTURES

1. **Ephesians 6:13** — Wherefore take unto you the whole armour of God, that ye may be able to withstand in the evil day, and having done all, to stand.

2. **Ephesians 6:14** — Stand therefore, having your loins girt about with truth, and having on the breastplate of righteousness.

3. **Ephesians 6:15** — And your feet shod with the preparation of the gospel of peace.

4. **Romans 5:1** — Therefore being justified by faith, we have peace with God through our Lord Jesus Christ.

5. **Romans 16:20** — And the God of peace shall bruise Satan under your feet shortly....

GREEK WORDS

1. "whole armour" — **πανοπλία** (*panoplia*): a compound of **πᾶν** (*pan*), meaning *all*, and **ὅπλον** (*hoplon*), which is the Greek word for weap-

onry; together, it means absolutely all the weaponry God has provided; pictures a soldier fully dressed in his armor from head to toe;
the full attire and weaponry of a soldier; the following hardware
was required for a soldier to be fully dressed for battle: the loin belt,
breastplate, shoes, shield, helmet, sword, and lance

2. "able" — **δύναμαι** (*dunamai*): depicts strength that makes one able,
capable, strong, and powerful; has power; has ability

3. "withstand" — **ἀντιστῆναι** (*antistenai*): to stand against; to push
against; to aggressively position oneself against

4. "evil" — **πονηρός** (*poneros*): malevolent, malicious, sinister, or wicked

5. "stand" — **στῆναι** (*stenai*): to stand; pictures a victorious soldier
standing upright

6. "stand" — **στῆτε** (*stete*): to stand upright; pictures one so confident
that he stands with his head held high and his shoulders thrown back

7. "shod" — **ὑποδέω** (*hupodeo*): a compound of the word **ὑπὸ** (*hupo*),
meaning under or underneath, and the word **δέω** (*deo*), which means
to bind or to tie up; pictures a shoe that is tightly bound or tied
around the foot

SYNOPSIS

We are instructed in Ephesians 6:13 to put on the whole armor of God
and to be clothed in the full weaponry we have available to us to defeat
the enemy. That includes keeping our feet shod with the Gospel of peace.
We must be determined to keep God's peace as a permanent fixture in our
daily lives.

The emphasis of this lesson:

**Before we were born again, we were at enmity with God. But now that
we have been redeemed and reconciled to God, we have two types of
peace available to us: peace *with* God and the peace *of* God. God's will is
for us to walk in peace in every area of life.**

Take Unto You the Whole Armor

Ephesians 6:13 says, "Wherefore take unto you the whole armour of God,
that ye may be able to withstand in the evil day, and having done all, to
stand." Notice, this verse does not instruct us to take unto ourselves "some"

of the armor or "our favorite piece" of the armor; it says we are to take up the *whole* armor of God.

The Greek word for "whole armour" is *panoplia*. It is a compound word made up of the words *pan*, which means *all*, and the word *haplos*, which is the word for *weapons*. When these two words are compounded, the word *panoplia* describes *full weaponry*.

When the apostle Paul wrote about the armor of God, he had these seven pieces of weaponry in mind.

1) his loin belt

2) his breastplate

3) his shoes

4) his shield

5) his sword

6) his helmet

7) his spears

Pressing Against the Enemy

Ephesians 6:13 says, "...that ye may be able to withstand in the evil day...." The phrase "that ye may be able" is the Greek word *dunamai*, and depicts *strength that makes one able, capable, strong, and powerful.* The Greek word for "stand" is *antistenai*, which is a compound word made up of the words *anti*, which means *against*, and *stenai*, which means *to stand*. It pictures a believer who is not in retreat but is pressing *against* the enemy. When we are dressed in the whole armor of God, we are in a position to put the devil on the run.

If the devil has tried to launch an attack against you or even just disrupt your day, you don't have to stand for it. According to Ephesians 6:13, we can stand against the "evil day." The word "evil," is a form of the Greek word *poneros*, which describes what is *malevolent, malicious, sinister*, or *wicked.* The "evil day" is any day you wake up and discover that something malevolent, malicious, wicked, or sinister is at work against you. But God has equipped you with everything you need to push evil back across the line and out of your day.

Redeemed, Purchased, and Transferred

Did you know evil has no place in your life? When you confessed Jesus as Lord, you were saved and redeemed. Jesus purchased you with His precious blood and rescued you from Satan's grip. Jesus not only made a way for you to spend eternity with Him, but He snatched you right out of the evil grasp of the enemy.

Colossians 1:13 says that God has "delivered us from the power of darkness, and hath translated us into the kingdom of his dear Son." And in the kingdom of His dear Son — where we now reside — there is no darkness; nothing in His kingdom is malevolent, malicious, wicked, or evil. If any of these powers of darkness try to disrupt our day, we can resist them; they don't belong! God has provided us with weapons we can use to push all evil out of our life.

You have the authority to deny access to every kind of evil that tries to infiltrate your life. Nothing is too big or too small. For instance, if you wake up one day feeling under the weather, you don't have to tolerate it; you can push it back over the line. But don't misunderstand; this does not mean there is no need for doctors or medication. If you need medication, you can take it. The point here is that you have access to more than just medication to fight any evil attack against your health. Available to you are all of the weapons found in the armor of God.

No matter what kind of attack is leveled your direction, you are divinely equipped to thwart *every* evil strategy set against you. Whether it is a headache, financial hardship, or trouble in a relationship, it does not belong in your life. And if evil is disrupting your day, you must use your God-given weapons and the authority you have in Christ to push them out.

An Ultimate Conclusion

Again, Ephesians 6:13 says, "Wherefore take unto you the whole armour of God, that ye may be able to withstand in the evil day, and *having done all, to stand.*" The original Greek text says, "And having brought the battle to an ultimate conclusion, stand."

When we are in the middle of a fight, it may be difficult to focus on anything other than the fight before us, but God knows the outcome; He knows who will be victorious in the end. He even knows what we will look like at the end of the fight. If we could see a snapshot of what we will look like on the other side, we would not see ourselves lying on the ground in a bloody heap with the devil standing on top of us! Rather, having brought the battle to an ultimate conclusion, *we* will be the one standing with the enemy under *our* feet!

Paul continued in verse 14 by saying, "Stand therefore...." The word "stand" is the Greek word *stenai* and means *to stand upright*. It pictures *one so confident that he stands with his head held high and his shoulders thrown back*. Paul was emphasizing that the reason we must stand up straight, hold our head high, throw our shoulders back, push our chest forward, and be proud of who we are in Christ is because we know the ultimate conclusion of the fight. We can be confident because we know we are fully equipped and *dressed to kill*!

The Shoes of a Roman Soldier

In Ephesians 6:15, we find the next piece of weaponry in the armor of God: "And your feet shod with the preparation of the gospel of peace." Traditionally, the shoes of a soldier began under the knee with a piece of metal that ran down to the ankle and wrapped around the leg. They were similar to a boot or tube of metal that covered the soldier's leg. Then around the foot were leather shoes very tightly bound around the foot on the bottom. The Roman soldier was to wrap the leather very tightly around his foot, and this was called having his feet "shod."

The word "shod" is made up of the Greek words *hupo* and *deo*. The word *hupo* means *under*, and *deo* means *to bind*. Together the words describe a shoe tightly bound around the foot. It was very important that the Roman soldier tied his shoes tightly because if he needed to move in battle and his shoes weren't tightly bound, he could walk right out of his shoes!

As believers, we must ensure that God's peace is a fixture in our life. We must tightly bind it to our feet so that we can walk in peace every day. Peace cannot be loosely fitted in our life; otherwise, we will walk right out of and lose our peace.

The Difference Between Peace *With* God and the Peace *of* God

There are two kinds of peace found in the Bible. The first is peace *with* God. This type of peace is mentioned in Romans 5:1, which says, "Being therefore justified by faith, we have peace with God through our Lord Jesus Christ." The apostle Paul taught in Colossians 1:21 and 22 that before we were saved, we were at enmity with God. God is holy; we were unholy. God is righteous; we were sinners. There was hostility between us and God.

But when we made Jesus the Lord of our life, the hostility between us and God was put away once and for all. Suddenly, as an act of His mercy and grace, we were put on the same side as God. All hostility and animosity were removed, and we became partners with God. More than that, we were given the birthright of a child of God. We have been reconciled to Him, and we now have peace *with* God (*see* Romans 5:10).

But there are many Christians who, although they have peace *with* God, don't have peace operating practically in their daily life. Many Christians worry, fret, and are anxious about things that will likely never happen. They are bombarded and tossed through life one way and another. They have peace with God but do not live in a *state* of peace. Instead, they live in a constant state of turmoil. It is possible to have peace with God, without experiencing a life of peace. As we saw in Colossians 1 and Romans 5, peace with God makes us right with Him, but the peace *of* God is a keeping peace.

Protected and Held in Place

Why did Paul liken the peace of God to the greaves, or shoes, of a Roman soldier? The answer becomes clear when we examine the three primary reasons the greaves were part of the soldier's armor.

1) Roman soldiers frequently walked over rocky terrain, and if their calves were not protected, they would be cut by the rocks.

2) Roman soldiers frequently walked through briar patches and thorns, and if their calves were not protected, they would be cut by the thorns.

3) Roman soldiers frequently faced enemies whose common tactic was to aim for the shins in an attempt to break the Roman soldier's legs. A strong kick to the shins could throttle a soldier to the ground, rendering him helpless and allowing the enemy to remove the Roman soldier's head. The greaves ensured that a kick from the enemy would have much less impact.

The same is true in our lives, spiritually speaking. As we walk through life, we can sometimes find ourselves in some "rocky" places. Beyond those rocky places, we may find ourselves in some very "thorny" situations. And in the worst situations, we can find that the enemy has taken us by surprise, "kicked us in the shins," and broken us.

However, when we are walking in the supernatural peace of God, it is as if we are walking in a divine "bubble." We don't seem to feel the rocks or thorns or sudden kicks from the enemy. It's as if we are insulated and unaffected by the enemy's assaults. And if we are impervious to the enemy's assaults, we can keep marching forward, and the enemy cannot stop us.

Peace can keep us moving forward despite the enemy's attacks, but another function of the peace of God is its ability to hold us in place. This is also perfectly illustrated by the shoes of a Roman soldier.

On the bottom of his shoes was where a soldier typically fixed long, sharp hobnails. Consequently, the greaves worn by Roman soldiers were similar to modern-day cleats. When a Roman soldier's feet were firmly planted in the ground, the enemy could push against him, but the soldier was nearly immovable. Likewise, any time the enemy tries to move us out of God's will, the peace of God will hold us in place.

With God's peace on our feet, we become like a palm tree in a hurricane. When hurricane winds blow, palm trees bend and nearly touch the ground. But when the hurricane subsides, the palm trees stand upright again. The trees are able to withstand the high-velocity winds because they are held in place by their roots. In the same way, when we have the peace of God, we are kept where we need to be. The enemy can push, push, and push against us, but the peace of God will hold us in place. The peace of God makes us *immovable*.

Killer Shoes

Along with keeping us moving forward and holding us in a place of faith, there is another major feature of the shoes of peace. Romans 16:20 says,

> **And the God of peace shall bruise Satan under your feet shortly....**

The word "bruise" describes the crushing of grapes by walking on them. It pictures the act of stepping on a grape with bare feet and feeling it squish underfoot. Another definition of the word "bruise" in the original Greek is *the crushing of bones*. We have been given the ability to crush Satan like bones under our feet!

The word "shortly" is associated with shoes because it describes the way the Roman soldiers marched in a parade formation. If someone stepped in front of the Roman soldier, the soldier would simply keep marching and knock the person flat. This would be detrimental for the person because of the hobnails on the bottoms of the soldiers' shoes.

Imagine what a person would look like after the soldiers passed over his body. They would have stomped and crushed and squished him under their feet. By saying, "…The God of peace shall bruise Satan under your feet shortly," Paul was indicating that if the devil is stupid enough to get in front of you, don't ask him to move; just keep marching. Make the devil regret he ever tried to resist you!

When you wear your shoes of peace, you are insulated from feeling the attacks of the enemy. In the face of peace, every demonic strategy falls apart and the devil's attacks only bounce off of you and fall useless to the ground. And on the bottom of your feet, you have the peace that holds you in place and enables you to keep moving forward. Even when the devil tries to stop you, you can keep marching forward and trample the devil with your *killer shoes*!

STUDY QUESTIONS

Study to shew thyself approved unto God, a workman that needeth not to be ashamed, rightly dividing the word of truth.
— 2 Timothy 2:15

1. Explain the Greek meaning of the phrase "that you may be able to stand" used in Ephesians 6:13.
2. Describe each part of the Roman soldier's shoes and the purpose of each part. How does each part relate to the life of a believer?
3. What is the "evil day" Paul mentioned in Ephesians 6:13? What is the believer's position of authority concerning the "evil day"?

PRACTICAL APPLICATION

**But be ye doers of the word, and not hearers only,
deceiving your own selves.**
—James 1:22

1. Consider your own life. Have you been living in worry and turmoil
    or in the peace of God? Read First Peter 5:7. What cares have you
    neglected to cast on Jesus?

2. Romans 16:20 says, "And the God of peace shall bruise Satan under
    your feet shortly...." If the devil is stupid enough to get in front of
    you, don't ask him to move; just keep marching. What can you do
    today to cast your cares on Him and "keep on marching"?

LESSON 13

TOPIC

The Shield of Faith

SCRIPTURES

1. **Ephesians 6:14** — Stand therefore, having your loins girt about with
    truth, and having on the breastplate of righteousness.

2. **Ephesians 6:15** — And your feet shod with the preparation of the
    gospel of peace

3. **Romans 6:16** — Above all, taking the shield of faith, wherewith ye
    shall be able to quench all the fiery darts of the wicked

4. **Romans 12:3** — For I say, through the grace given unto me, to every
    man that is among you, not to think of himself more highly than he
    ought to think; but to think soberly, according as God hath dealt to
    every man the measure of faith

5. **Romans 10:17** — So then faith cometh by hearing, and hearing by
    the word of God

GREEK WORDS

1. "stand" — **στῆναι** (*stenai*): to stand; pictures a victorious soldier
    standing upright

2. "therefore" — **οὖν** (*oun*): a conjunction; consequently; accordingly; hence; as a result
3. "wicked" — **πονηρός** (*poneros*): insidious, malevolent, or wicked

SYNOPSIS

After the belt of truth, the breastplate of righteousness, and the shoes of peace, the next weapon Paul listed in Ephesians 6 as part of the armor of God is the shield of faith. Paul wrote many of his epistles while he was in prison. Much of his time in confinement was spent chained to a Roman guard, and in such close quarters, Paul could easily observe the soldier's helmet, breastplate, shield, sword, lance, and shoes. It's clear to see that the Holy Spirit began to speak to Paul through his environment, giving Paul a revelation about how the soldier's natural weapons were comparable to the spiritual weapons God has given us.

The emphasis of this lesson:

There are many similarities between the shield of faith and the ancient Roman battle shield. A diligent Roman soldier took special care of his shield daily to ensure it would always be battle ready and in peak condition. Likewise, there are things we must do to ensure our faith is always positioned in front of us, effectively quenching all the fiery darts of the enemy.

As we learned in previous lessons, the first epistle written by the apostle Paul was the book of First Thessalonians. In this epistle, Paul listed some weaponry of the Holy Spirit, but it was an under-developed list. Years later, by the time Paul wrote the book of Ephesians, his revelation on the subject of spiritual armor had grown, and he recorded his full revelation of the armor of God in Ephesians 6.

We also learned in previous lessons that the apostle Paul wrote many of his epistles while he was in prison. Much of his time in confinement was spent chained to a Roman guard, and in such close quarters, Paul could easily observe the soldier's helmet, breastplate, shield, sword, lance, and shoes. It's clear to see that the Holy Spirit began to speak to Paul through his environment, giving Paul a revelation about how the soldier's natural weapons were comparable to the spiritual weapons God has given us.

After encouraging the Ephesian church to take up the whole armor of God so they would be able to withstand evil, Paul wrote in Ephesians 6:14, "Stand therefore…." The word "stand" pictures *a Roman soldier standing erect with his back completely straight, his shoulders thrown back, his chest out, and his head held high.* It pictures *someone who is completely confident* and depicts *a soldier who is dressed, equipped, and has no reason to be afraid.* When we are dressed in the whole armor of God, we can stand tall and walk in full confidence.

The Greek word for "therefore" is *oun* and is better translated *consequently* or *as a result.* Paul was essentially saying in Ephesians 6:13 and 14, "…Take up the whole armor of God, that you may be able to withstand in the evil day, and having done all, to stand. As a result, stand tall, hold your head high, and throw your shoulders back."

The Shoes of Peace

In Ephesians 6:14 and 15, Paul continued to encourage the church at Ephesus by beginning to list the spiritual weaponry that is available to believers. The first three weapons Paul mentioned were the loin belt of truth, the breastplate of righteousness, and the shoes of peace.

Verse 15 says, "And your feet shod with the preparation of the gospel of peace." The Roman soldier's shoes protected not only his feet but his shins. If a soldier needed to walk through rocky or thorny terrain, his shins would be protected against cuts, scrapes, and bruises. Additionally, during a battle situation, the enemy would often attempt to incapacitate the Roman soldier by kicking him in the shins and breaking his legs. But with the Roman soldier's shoes, or greaves, on his feet, he could walk through any terrain unscathed and withstand any deadly kicks from the enemy.

Likewise, when we walk in the supernatural peace of God, we are protected; it is as if we are walking in a divine "bubble," insulated from the enemy's attacks. The devil hates this because even though he launches attacks that take us through "rocky" or "thorny" situations, we can remain in a bubble of divine protection. Even if the enemy tries to surprise us with a debilitating "kick" that could leave us broken, God's peace insulates us. We have the ability to be unaffected by turmoil and unmoved by surprise enemy attacks because the peace of God gives us the power to keep moving forward.

But in addition to keeping us moving forward, the peace of God can also keep us firmly planted in faith. When we are living in God's peace, we are like a sturdy palm tree with deep, strong roots. During a hurricane, a palm tree can withstand the winds and bend without breaking because it has deep roots that keep the tree planted. We may bend under the devil's attacks, but with the peace of God, we will not break, because God's peace holds us in faith. And just like the palm tree, when the winds of turmoil stop blowing, we will rise right back into place.

In our previous lesson, we also studied Romans 16:20, which says, "And the God of peace shall bruise Satan under your feet *shortly*." The Greek readers of Paul's day understood the meaning of this passage because of the word "shortly." This is a very specific word describing the stomping motion of Roman soldiers as they marched in formation.

In the original Greek, the word for "bruise" was used in two ways. First, it was used to describe *the smashing of grapes into wine*. Secondly, it was used to describe *the crushing of bones into powder*. Romans 16:20 tells us the devil will be crushed like bones into powder under our feet. Notice this crushing takes place under *our* feet, not under God's feet!

In the previous lesson, we also learned that the Roman soldier's shoes had sharp hobnails fixed to the bottom that could be used to deliver a deadly kick to the enemy or to trample anyone who got in the way. These were killer shoes!

Imagine an entire squadron of Roman soldiers marching in formation, as described by the use of the word "shortly" in Romans 16:20. As these soldiers are marching, pounding and stomping on the pavement, they are making their presence known. What would happen if someone stepped in the path of these soldiers? Rather than politely asking the person to move out of the way, those Roman soldiers would keep stomping and marching forward, and anything or anyone in their way would be crushed under their feet, leaving that person in a bloody mess!

That is the image described in Romans 16:20 when the apostle Paul said, "And the God of peace shall bruise Satan under your feet shortly." If the devil is dumb enough to get in our way, then our response should be to keep pressing forward. The peace of God enables us to trample the devil under our feet and keep marching along. *That is powerful!*

The Shield of Faith

After the belt of truth, the breastplate of righteousness, and the shoes of peace, the next weapon Paul listed as part of the armor of God is the shield of faith. Ephesians 6:16 says,

Above all, taking the shield of faith, wherewith ye shall be able to quench all the fiery darts of the wicked.

Notice the *King James Version* begins verse 16 by using the phrase "Above all." Some people have misunderstood it to mean that faith is the most important weapon in our arsenal, but this is not a good translation. A better translation of the original Greek wording would be "covering all." It describes the *position* of faith and explains why Paul likened it to a shield.

Among the Roman soldiers there were two kinds of shields: the *aspis* and the *thyreon*. Roman soldiers who were marching in a parade through a town or city carried a round shield, or *aspis*, that was beautifully ornate and would never be carried into battle. The battle shield was called a *thyreon*, which is the very same word to describe *any door in a house*. The *thyreon* was very heavy, and it was so large that, if used correctly, it covered the soldier on all sides.

The exterior of the Roman battle shield was made from wood, and the interior was made from seven layers of animal hide that caused the shield to be nearly as impenetrable as steel. Over time, however, if the leather was not treated properly, it could become hard and eventually brittle. Once the leather became brittle, it was breakable and could be easily penetrated by enemy weapons.

In order to avoid his shield leather becoming brittle, the Roman soldier had a strict daily regimen to ensure his shield remained in its best possible condition. Every morning, the first thing a responsible soldier would do was care for the leather interior of his shield. He would douse a rag with oil then massage the oil into the leather to make sure it never became hard or brittle. If a soldier wanted to keep his shield in good shape, he had to regularly anoint his shield with oil. In the same way, to keep our faith from becoming dry and brittle, we must regularly apply "oil" to it, keeping our faith in its best possible condition.

In Scripture, the word "oil" often represents the Holy Spirit. Knowing what we do about what was required in order to maintain a physical

Roman shield, we can understand that our spiritual shield of faith cannot properly defend us if we do not regularly encounter the Holy Spirit. We cannot run on faith from the past; we need faith that is regularly anointed by and submitted to the Holy Spirit.

How To Grow in Faith

Some may feel discouraged in their faith and say, "I just don't have as much faith as everyone else." But Romans 12:3 says "…God hath dealt to *every* man the measure of faith." This means God has not granted more faith to certain people and less faith to others. No, He has given *every person* the same amount of faith.

But we do have the ability to *grow* our faith! Romans 10:17 tells us how to do it: "…Faith comes by hearing, and hearing by the word of God." When we hear the Word of God over and over, faith comes. We all start with "the measure of faith," but it can be developed, grown, and strengthened through hearing the Word of God.

Romans 4 describes how Abraham grew in faith. Abraham began with the same amount of faith as everyone else, but he grew his faith by continuously hearing the word he received from God. Likewise, if we want our faith to become tougher and stronger and also want it to grow, we need to be regularly subjected to good Bible teaching. Bombarding our ears with the Word of God will cause our faith to grow!

How To Quench Fiery Darts

Another battle-strategy of the Roman soldier was to take his shield and submerge it in a river or a pond. He would leave it under the water until all seven layers of hide were completely saturated and the shield became very heavy. But there was a very good reason for this practice. Ephesians 6:16 explains it this way:

> **…Wherewith ye shall be able to quench all the fiery darts of the wicked.**

When the Roman soldier's shield was water-soaked, not only would it function in the typical way, causing arrows to ricochet away from the soldier, but if a flaming arrow was launched at him, the water in his shield would extinguish the flames. Every soldier knew that if he was going to get the best use of his shield, it would need to be water-soaked.

Likewise, we should consistently "soak" our faith in the water of the Word of God (*see* Ephesians 5:26). When we consistently hear the Word, our faith becomes more and more effective because it is saturated in Truth. When the enemy sends his volley of fiery arrows your way, your faith will extinguish the flames, rendering them ineffective.

Ephesians 6:16 continues, "...You will be able to quench all the fiery darts of the wicked." The word "wicked" describes whatever is *malevolent* or *insidious*. The original Greek word for "fiery darts" described long, slender arrows that looked like normal arrows but were hollow inside. Ancient soldiers would fill the arrows with combustible fluid, and even though it appeared normal, it would burst into flames upon impact. These arrows were like torpedoes in the air!

Many times, when the devil attacks, we don't know how serious it is until impact. But if we have maintained our shield of faith, regularly anointing it with a fresh dose of the Holy Ghost and soaking it in the Word of God, the enemy can send these flaming arrows against us, and our faith will extinguish the flame.

STUDY QUESTIONS

Study to shew thyself approved unto God, a workman that needeth not to be ashamed, rightly dividing the word of truth.
— 2 Timothy 2:15

1. Describe the difference between the round shield and the oblong shield of the Roman soldier. Why do you think Paul likened our faith to the Roman battle shield?

2. Read Romans 12:3. According to this verse, how can a person grow his faith?

PRACTICAL APPLICATION

But be ye doers of the word, and not hearers only, deceiving your own selves.
— James 1:22

1. In the same way a soldier regularly applied oil to his shield, we must regularly apply "oil" to our faith to keep it from getting dry and brittle. Have you ever experienced a time when your faith seemed dry or

easily broken? What did you do to apply the oil of the Holy Spirit to your faith and get it back to a battle-ready condition?

2. Every soldier knew that if he was going to get the best use of his shield, it would need to be water-soaked. Consider your own life. Do you daily fortify your faith with the Word of God? Are you prioritizing the Scriptures? How can you make more time in your daily life for more time spent in God's Word?

LESSON 14

TOPIC

The Helmet of Salvation

SCRIPTURES

1. **Ephesians 6:14,15** — Stand therefore, having your loins girt about with truth, and having on the breastplate of righteousness; and your feet shod with the preparation of the gospel of peace

2. **Ephesians 6:16** — Above all, taking the shield of faith, wherewith ye shall be able to quench all the fiery darts of the wicked.

3. **Ephesians 6:17** — And take the helmet of salvation, and the sword of the Spirit, which is the word of God:

GREEK WORDS

1. "helmet" — **περικεφαλαία** (*perikephalaia*): compound of **περι** (*peri*) and **κεφαλή** (*kephale*); the word **περι** (*peri*) means around, and **κεφαλή** (*kephale*) means the head; compounded, it denotes a piece of armor that fits very tightly around the head

2. "salvation" — **σωτηρία** (*soteria*): salvation or deliverance; a state of deliverance, healing, and wholeness; conveys the idea of wholeness in every part of life; pictures prosperity, deliverance, protection, soundness of mind, and physical healing; expresses the ideas of present deliverance, healing, preservation, prosperity, safety, and general welfare

SYNOPSIS

The Roman soldier's helmet was the most ornately decorated and noticeable piece of weaponry he possessed and an integral part of his armor. On top of being beautiful, the Roman helmet protected against the advances of the enemy, who often carried a battle axe; without it, the soldier could have *literally* lost his head. In the same way, your salvation is the most noticeable thing in your life, and it protects your mind from evil attacks against your precious, all-encompassing salvation.

The emphasis of this lesson:

If allowed, the enemy will use his spiritual "battle axe" to whack away at our thinking and convince us to relinquish our belief in the benefits of our salvation. What we believe determines what we receive, so we must be determined to protect our mind and believe God's Word concerning all that is included in the salvation Jesus purchased for us on the Cross.

We have been studying the spiritual weaponry God has provided to all believers as described by Paul in Ephesians 6. In previous lessons, we learned about the belt of truth, the breastplate of righteousness, the shoes of peace, and the shield of faith that protects us against the fiery darts of the enemy. Ephesians 6:14-16 says:

> **Stand therefore, having your loins girt about with truth, and having on the breastplate of righteousness; and your feet shod with the preparation of the gospel of peace; above all, taking the shield of faith, wherewith ye shall be able to quench all the fiery darts of the wicked.**

Each piece of natural weaponry had a specific purpose, and there was a reason why Paul chose to associate each natural weapon with a particular spiritual weapon. Let's review why Paul likened our faith to the Roman battle shield.

The Shield of Faith

Paul wrote that above all, we are to take up the shield of faith to quench the "fiery darts" of the enemy. The phrase, "fiery darts" is the same phrase used by the ancient historian Thucydides when he described long, slender arrows that looked like normal arrows, but were hollow inside and filled with combustible fluid. Before impact, they looked like simple arrows, but once they reached their target and made contact, they would explode.

To counteract this strategy, the Roman soldier would take his shield and submerge it in a river or a pond. He would leave it under the water until it was completely saturated, and the shield became very heavy. Once the shield was completely soaked, not only would it function in the typical way, causing arrows to ricochet away from the soldier, but if a flaming arrow was launched at him, the water in his shield would extinguish the flame.

There are times when the enemy sends "fiery darts" our way, but if we have our shield of faith in front of us, those fiery darts will simply ricochet off or be totally extinguished. If we consistently saturate our faith in the Word of God, the fiery darts of the enemy cannot penetrate our shield.

The Helmet of Salvation

The next piece of weaponry Paul mentioned in Ephesians 6 is found in verse 17, which says "And take the helmet of salvation…." To bring more light to the reason Paul likened our salvation to a helmet, Rick shared and excerpt from his book, *Dressed to Kill*:

> The Roman soldier's helmet was a fascinating and beautiful part of his armor. It was a flamboyant piece of weaponry, very ornate and intricate. In fact, it looked more like a piece of artwork than a helmet! Rather than being a simple piece of metal formed to fit his head, the Roman soldier's helmet was highly decorated with all kinds of engravings and etchings….

> Furthermore, as if these fabulous engravings and etchings were not enough, a huge plume of brightly colored feathers or horse-hair stood straight up out of the top of the helmet. If the helmet was one to be used in a public ceremony or parade, this brightly colored plume could be very long — long enough to hang all the way down the soldier's back.

> The helmet was made of bronze and equipped with pieces of armor that were specifically designed to protect the cheeks and jaws. It was extremely heavy; therefore, the interior of the helmet was lined with a spongy material in order to soften its weight upon the soldier's head. This piece of armor was so strong, so

massive, and so heavy that nothing could pierce it — not even a hammer or a battleaxe.

The helmet of the Roman soldier was designed to protect the back of his neck from the enemy. If given the opportunity, the enemy would take the soldier's head right off of his shoulders. *The helmet was so important!*

The Roman soldier's helmet was the most noticeable piece of weaponry that he possessed. The breastplate was dazzling, but it would have been extremely intimidating to approach a soldier wearing a helmet with a bright plume of horsehair cascading down from the top. Likewise, your salvation is a beautiful gift from God! Your salvation is the most noticeable thing in your life. When you confidently wear your helmet and walk in your salvation, you are *noticeable!*

The Benefits of Salvation

The word "helmet" is taken from the Word *perikephalaia*. The word *peri* means *around* and the word *kephale* is the Greek word for *the head*. When these two words are compounded, the new word *perikephalaia* denotes a piece of armor that fits very tightly around the head. Paul was indicating that just as a helmet was fitted tightly around a soldier's head, our salvation should fit tightly around our mind.

If we do not hold fast to our salvation, the devil will begin to hack away at our minds, causing us to loosen the grip of faith we have on all the benefits that were purchased for us through Jesus' act of salvation. Jesus not only saved us from an eternity in hell, but He made sure we could live a victorious life here on the earth. The Greek word for "salvation" is *soterios*, which includes prosperity, deliverance, protection, soundness of mind, and even physical healing.

The devil does not want us to enjoy any of these benefits. So if we do not firmly wrap around our mind what belongs to us in Christ, the devil will come to attack our minds through wrong preaching, the opinions of friends, or the voices of people we look up to.

If given access, the devil will begin to relentlessly attack our thoughts, trying to convince us that prosperity is not truly involved in our salvation. If he is continually allowed access to our mind, he will totally axe our belief in the prosperous life Jesus wants us to have, and we will tragically lose the prosperity that belongs to us.

The enemy will also come against our promise of healing by trying to convince us that physical healing does not belong to us in salvation. He will propose that only spiritual healing belongs to us. But, friend, this is not true. The Bible tells us that we have been *spiritually raised from the dead*, not spiritually healed. When we confess Jesus as Lord, we are *resurrected*.

If allowed access, the enemy will continue to whack at our understanding of salvation until, finally, we no longer even believe in the benefits of salvation at all. The enemy will repeatedly swing his spiritual battle axe against God's truth about our salvation until we no longer believe in the possibility of having a sound mind!

The devil will continue to attack our thinking until he leaves us nothing but the hope of Heaven. We praise God for the hope of Heaven, but we are not in Heaven at this moment; we are in this world where we need healing, prosperity, and soundness of mind. We need everything Jesus died to give us in this life.

Paul exhorted us to put on the helmet of salvation and said we must have that helmet tightly wrapped around our head. He understood that the devil always comes with his battle axe and does everything he can to whack every benefit of our salvation away from us. Left unchecked, the enemy will leave us with nothing but hope for Heaven.

But the helmet of our salvation does so much more than offer hope for the future. It gives us a weapon we can use *today* so we can walk in victory *now* by protecting our thoughts and beliefs. Without it, we can lose our soundness of mind, forfeit our physical healing, and no longer believe in prosperity. What we believe determines what we receive. If we don't believe correctly, we will not receive the good things in our lives that God has intended. We may still believe in Heaven, but the enemy will use his spiritual battle axe to whack the rest of the benefits of salvation out of our mind.

So how do we guard against this type of attack and ensure that our helmet of salvation stays fitly in place? We must spend time studying what the Bible says about healing, deliverance from evil powers, and redemption and its beneficial consequences in our life. When our heart is full of the Word of God, we begin to speak the Word of God. And when we speak the Word, we believe the Word. That is how we protect our belief in the truth and keep our helmet of salvation securely in place.

The Power To 'Put On' the Armor

Ephesians 6:11 says we are to "put on the whole armour of God...." The Greek word for "put on" is *enduo*, a compound of *en* and *dunamis*. The word *en* means *into*, and *dunamis* means *supernatural power* or *dynamic power*, and it was used to describe *forces of nature like an earthquake, a tornado, or a hurricane*. This means that when we receive the supernatural power of God, it dresses us in the weaponry Paul described in Ephesians 6.

The whole armor of God is necessary, but our salvation is a masterpiece; it is the most noticeable gift in our life. And when we really embrace salvation and all of the benefits it entails, we will stand out from among the crowd. The power of God in operation in our life will cause people to look at us and say, "There is something different about that person."

As long as we are walking in that *dunamis* power, it puts a helmet on our head, secures a breastplate on our chest, wraps a loin belt around us, puts greaves on our shins, and fits killer shoes on our feet. His power also puts a shield in one hand and a sword in the other and gives us a spear to use against the enemy from a distance. As long as we continue to walk in the power of God, we are dressed in all that the weaponry of God provides.

STUDY QUESTIONS

> Study to shew thyself approved unto God, a workman that needeth
> not to be ashamed, rightly dividing the word of truth.
> — 2 Timothy 2:15

1. Describe the ancient Roman soldier's helmet and how it is a spiritual picture of our helmet of salvation.
2. The Greek word for "salvation" is *soterios*. What are the benefits included in this word?

PRACTICAL APPLICATION

> But be ye doers of the word, and not hearers only,
> deceiving your own selves.
> — James 1:22

1. Identify an area in your life where you have neglected to walk in the full benefits of your salvation. Find one scripture that will strengthen you in the area you have identified.

2. Romans 12:2 says, "And be not conformed to this world: but be ye transformed by the renewing of your mind, that ye may prove what is that good, and acceptable, and perfect, will of God." How does what you learned about the helmet of salvation impact your understanding of this verse? How will you apply it to your life today?

LESSON 15

TOPIC

The Sword of the Spirit

SCRIPTURES

1. **Ephesians 6:14,15** — Stand therefore, having your loins girt about with truth, and having on the breastplate of righteousness; and your feet shod with the preparation of the gospel of peace.

2. **Ephesians 6:16** — Above all, taking the shield of faith, wherewith ye shall be able to quench all the fiery darts of the wicked.

3. **Ephesians 6:17** — And take the helmet of salvation, and the sword of the Spirit, which is the word of God.

4. **Hebrews 4:12** — For the word of God is quick, and powerful, and sharper than any twoedged sword....

5. **Matthew 4:1-7** — Then was Jesus led up of the Spirit into the wilderness to be tempted of the devil. And when he had fasted forty days and forty nights, he was afterward an hungered. And when the tempter came to him, he said, If thou be the Son of God, command that these stones be made bread. But he answered and said, It is written, Man shall not live by bread alone, but by every word that proceedeth out of the mouth of God. Then the devil taketh him up into the holy city, and setteth him on a pinnacle of the temple, and saith unto him, If thou be the Son of God, cast thyself down: for it is written, He shall give his angels charge concerning thee: and in their hands they shall bear thee up, lest at any time thou dash thy foot against a stone. Jesus said unto him, It is written again, Thou shalt not tempt the Lord thy God

GREEK WORDS

1. "sword" — μάχαιρα (*machaira*): a sword that was an exceptionally brutal weapon; it most often was shorter and shaped like a dagger; a sword used for close-range stabbing; a deadly and frightful weapon that nearly always inflicted a fatal wound

2. "word" — ῥῆμα (*rhema*): a fresh, clear, specific spoken word; a suddenly quickened word

3. "two-edged" — δίστομος (*distomos*): compound of δίς (*dis*), meaning two, and στόμα (*stoma*), which means mouth; a two-mouthed sword

SYNOPSIS

The sword of the Spirit Paul spoke of in Ephesians 6 was based on the Roman soldier's sword, which was short and used for stabbing the enemy at close range. We have also been given a sword to use against the enemy at close range; it is called the Word of God.

The emphasis of this lesson:

We have been given a powerful weapon to repel Satan's every attack against us — the sword of the Spirit, which is the Word, or *rhema*, of God. But a *rhema* word is not simply picking up your Bible and choosing something you want to read. We must learn to properly and effectively wield the sword of the Spirit so that we are able to defend ourselves against the attacks of the enemy.

In Ephesians 6:14-17, Paul began to describe the spiritual weapons God has made available to every believer:

> **Stand therefore, having your loins gird about with truth, and having on the breastplate of righteousness; and your feet shod with the preparation of the gospel of peace; above all, taking the shield of faith, wherewith ye shall be able to quench all the fiery darts of the wicked. And take the helmet of salvation, and the sword of the Spirit, which is the word of God.**

In previous lessons, we learned about the belt of truth, the breastplate of righteousness, the shoes of peace, the shield of faith, and the helmet of salvation that protects our mind from the enemy's attacks against our belief. In this lesson, we will dive into why Paul chose the Roman sword as a comparison to the Word of God.

The *Machaira* Sword

On the program, Rick read an excerpt from his book, *Dressed To Kill*, to bring more context to our understanding of the sword of the Spirit.

When he [Paul] wrote, "…and the sword of the Spirit, which is the word of God," the word for "sword," as used in this text, comes from the Greek word *machaira*.

The *machaira* was approximately 19 to 22 inches long with a very sharp blade. It was relatively light, easy to carry, and used for close-range thrusting. This sword was carried in a scabbard and was designed to inflict a mortal wound on an enemy or an aggressor.

The *machaira* was an exceptionally brutal weapon. Both sides of its blade were razor sharp, making this sword extremely dangerous when used in the hands of a well-trained soldier. It was a weapon of murder. This is the sword Paul had in mind when he wrote about spiritual armor in Ephesians 6:17.

As mentioned in the excerpt from *Dressed To Kill*, the *machaira* was a two-edged sword, and both edges were extremely sharp. These swords were not very long because they were used for thrusting and ultimately stabbing the enemy. This was the type of sword Paul had in mind when he wrote about our spiritual sword of the Spirit.

A Rhema Word

Paul said in Ephesians 6:17, "…and the sword of the Spirit, which is the word of God." In the Greek language, the word "word" is *rhema*. This word describes something that is *spoken clearly, vividly, and in undeniable language* or *spoken in unmistakable, unquestionable, certain, and definite terms*. In the New Testament, the word *rhema* carries the idea of *a quickened word, a word of Scripture*, or *a word from the Lord that the Holy Spirit supernaturally drops into a believer's heart*. When a believer receives a *rhema* word from the Spirit of God, that word comes alive to impart special power or direction to that believer.

These *rhema* words are powerful and give us sword-power — the ability to stab the enemy. When the Holy Spirit supernaturally quickens such a word or a specific Bible verse to a believer's heart and mind, that believer *unquestionably* knows that what he has heard is from the Lord. Suddenly, he has power to thrust that "sword" into the enemy that is trying to attack him.

A *rhema* word is not simply picking up your Bible and choosing something you want to read. A *rhema* word is something that is quickened on the inside of you. It is a promise from the Bible or even a prophetic word that has been quickened, or made alive, within you. Many times, this looks like the Holy Spirit supernaturally reminding you of a scripture or Bible promise. One expositor has translated Ephesians 6:17 this way: "...the sword that the Spirit wields as he draws forth a special word from God...."

When this happens, that word, scripture, or promise floods our entire being with faith because the Holy Spirit has communicated it to us in a way that is *clearly spoken, unmistakable, undeniable, unquestionable, certain,* and *definite.* Thus, a *rhema* word is a specific word or message that the Holy Spirit quickens in our hearts and minds at a specific time for a special purpose. When Paul described the sword of the Spirit, which is the Word of God, he was referring to the Holy Spirit's ability to make such a divine word come vividly alive in our hearts and minds in a moment of need.

The Central Piece of Weaponry

As we have studied in previous lessons, every Roman soldier had a central piece of weaponry called the loin belt. We learned that the loin belt was wrapped around the waist of the soldier, holding all of the other pieces of weaponry together and protecting his loins, or reproductive abilities. We also learned that the loin belt of truth refers to the Word of God — the Bible. And in Ephesians 6:14, Paul made it clear that the *truth* is as central to our spiritual weaponry as the loin belt was to the Roman soldier's physical weaponry.

On either side of the Roman loin belt, there was a clip. One clip held the shield and the other held the sword. The Apostle Paul likened the Roman shield to our faith, calling it the "shield of faith" because he wanted us to understand that if we want our faith to be effective, we must keep it connected to the Word of God.

The clip on the other side of the loin belt held the scabbard that held the *machaira* sword — a double-edged sword. Paul likened the Roman sword to the *rhema* word of God because he wanted us to understand that any *rhema* word we receive will be rooted in the Bible.

When a *rhema* word comes to us, it is usually while we are reading the Bible or reflecting on Scripture. We may be reading a verse when, suddenly, we see with brand new eyes a verse we have read many times before. The verse then supernaturally comes alive in us and is exactly what we have been searching for. We receive an answer we need — a *rhema* word from God.

The Source of a Rhema Word

As we've seen before, the loin belt is representative of the written Word of God — the Bible — which is the primary source for a genuine *rhema* from God. In the same way the loin belt was the central piece of weaponry that held everything together and was the piece on which the sword and spear hung, the Bible holds our spiritual armor together and is the truth on which every word from God hangs.

The apostle Paul likened a *rhema* word from God to a sword because when we receive such a word, it is as if God has put a supernatural sword in our hand. A *rhema* word is a powerful weapon with which to repel Satan's attacks against us, and it is supernaturally empowered by the Holy Spirit. But it is not enough to simply *have* a sword, we must know how to *wield* it. To know that, we must learn more about the double-edged sword Paul was referring to in Ephesians 6.

A Two-Mouthed Sword

There are many references in the Bible to a double-edged sword. In Revelation 1:16, John, while he was on the Isle of Patmos, described Jesus as having a double-edged sword coming out of His mouth. Revelation 2:13 also describes Jesus with a double-edged sword. Hebrews 4:12 says, "For the Word of God is quick, powerful, and sharper than any two-edged sword.

We know from Ephesians 6:18, the Word of God is the double-edged sword of the Spirit. In the original Greek text, the word for "double-edged" is *distomos*. The word *di* means *two* and the word *stomos* is the Greek word for "the mouth." The literal translation is *a two-mouthed sword*.

When the Word of God comes out of the mouth of God, it has one edge to the blade. And when that word drops down into our heart and we begin to meditate on it, suddenly, the Holy Spirit quickens it to us, and it becomes a weapon that can be used against the enemy.

When that word comes out of your mouth — the second mouth — it adds a second edge to the sword. It doesn't become a two-edged sword until it comes out of two mouths — first God's, then yours. There is nothing more deadly than a two-edged sword!

Jesus' Two-Mouthed Sword

Then was Jesus led up of the Spirit into the wilderness to be tempted of the devil. And when He had fasted forty days and forty nights, he was afterward an hungered. And when the tempter came to him, he said, If thou be the Son of God, command that these stones be made bread. But he [Jesus] answered and said, It is written, Man shall not live by bread alone, but by every word that proceedeth out of the mouth of God.

— Matthew 4:1-4

Jesus had been fasting in the wilderness when he was assaulted by the enemy, and His response to the attack was to speak the Word of God. God provided the first edge of the sword when He first spoke His Word, then when it came out of Jesus' mouth, it added a second edge to the blade — and it was *powerful*. The Holy Spirit quickened within Jesus the verse Deuteronomy 8:3, and Jesus spoke it out, saying, "It is written, Man shall not live by bread alone, but by every word that proceedeth out of the mouth of God."

But the enemy wasn't finished with Jesus; he attacked again:

Then the devil taketh him up into the holy City, and setteth him on a pinnacle of the temple, and saith unto him, If thou be the Son of God, cast thyself down: for it is written, He shall give his angels charge concerning thee: and in their hands they shall bear thee up, lest at any time thou dash thy foot against a stone. Jesus said unto him, It is written again, Thou shalt not tempt the Lord thy God.

— Matthew 4:5-7

In that very moment, the Holy Spirit quickened in Jesus the exact promise or scripture Jesus needed to use. God had already provided the first edge of the sword when He first spoke His Word, then when Jesus said, "Thou shalt not tempt the Lord thy God," it added a second edge to the blade, making it double-edged like the *machaira* sword.

Jesus responded to every attack the same way — by speaking the Word of God as the Spirit quickened it in His heart. The devil attacked a third and final time, and after Jesus' response, he left Jesus (*see* v. 11). In this encounter with the enemy, Jesus perfectly demonstrated the power of the Sword of the Spirit and how to use it.

When we receive a word from God, we must do what Jesus did and speak it out of our mouth. But we must remember that every *rhema* Word we need will primarily come out of the loin belt of truth, which is the Bible. If we do not consistently read the Bible and meditate on God's Word, we will have a difficult time recognizing and receiving a *rhema* word from the Holy Spirit. But if we spend time reading the Word of God, the Holy Spirit will quicken in our heart exactly what we need — the double-edged sword of the Spirit.

Earlier in this lesson we learned that the *machaira* sword was used for thrusting at close range. It was used when the enemy was close. Similarly, when we are in close combat with the enemy or in the midst of intense, difficult situations, this is the very moment the Holy Spirit will give us a *rhema* Word for thrusting at the enemy at close range.

There is a spiritual sword available to us — the *rhema* word of God — and when we receive it, we suddenly have sword-power to stab the enemy whenever he comes against us. The Holy Spirit wants to put this sword in our hand, but we must wield it by speaking out the Word of God when He quickens it in our heart!

STUDY QUESTIONS

Study to shew thyself approved unto God, a workman that needeth not to be ashamed, rightly dividing the word of truth.
— 2 Timothy 2:15

1. Describe the *machaira* sword Paul wrote about in Ephesians 6:17 and explain why its design was significant.
2. Explain in your own words a *rhema* word of God.
3. How is the loin belt, or the Bible, central to all of the other weaponry God has made accessible to us?

PRACTICAL APPLICATION

**But be ye doers of the word, and not hearers only,
deceiving your own selves.
—James 1:22**

1. Have you ever received a *rhema* word from God? If so, describe the experience and the impact it had on your personal life. If not, what steps will you take to ensure you are prepared to recognize and receive a *rhema* word from the Holy Spirit?

2. The Word of God is a sword, but it becomes a *double-edged* sword when it comes out of your mouth. Describe a time when you spoke the Word of God concerning a particular situation and saw that situation turn around for your good. If you have never experienced this, consider a troubling circumstance you may be going through right now. Take some time today to pray and ask the Holy Spirit for a solution. Then take a few minutes to read some verses in the Bible that apply to your situation and write down the ones(s) that seem to "drop down" into your heart. Then consistently speak those verses out of your mouth concerning your situation until you know what steps to take, or you see a miracle!

LESSON 16

TOPIC

The Lance of Intercession

SCRIPTURES

1. **Ephesians 6:14-17** — Stand therefore, having your loins girt about with truth, and having on the breastplate of righteousness; and your feet shod with the preparation of the gospel of peace. Above all, taking the shield of faith, wherewith ye shall be able to quench all the fiery darts of the wicked. And take the helmet of salvation, and the sword of the Spirit, which is the word of God.

2. **Ephesians 6:13** — Wherefore take unto you the whole armour of God....

3. **Ephesians 6:18** — Praying always with all prayer and supplication in the Spirit, and watching thereunto with all perseverance and supplication for all saints.

GREEK WORDS

1. "whole armour" — **πανοπλία** (*panoplia*): a compound of **πᾶν** (*pan*), meaning all, and **ὅπλον** (*hoplon*), which is the Greek word for weaponry; together, it means absolutely all the weaponry God has provided; it pictures a soldier fully dressed in his armor from head to toe; the full attire and weaponry of a soldier; the following hardware was required for a soldier to be fully dressed for battle: the loin belt, breastplate, shoes, shield, helmet, sword, and lance

SYNOPSIS

Each piece of spiritual weaponry is essential to walking successfully through every attack of the enemy. The seventh and final piece of spiritual weaponry listed in Ephesians 6 is the lance of prayer. The physical lance of ancient Rome came in various sizes, and Paul taught that, similarly, there are many different kinds of prayer as well.

The emphasis of this lesson:

The Roman soldier carried many lances of various sizes in a pouch that was attached to his loin belt. Once again, we see how the loin belt of truth — the written Word of God — is the central piece of weaponry on which every other weapon depends.

The *Whole* Armor of God

We have been studying Ephesians 6, where the spiritual weapons that have been made available to us are listed. Let's begin this lesson in Ephesians 6:14-17, which says:

> **Stand therefore, having your loins girt about with truth, and having on the breastplate of righteousness; and your feet shod with the preparation of the gospel of peace; Above all, taking the shield of faith, wherewith ye shall be able to quench all the fiery darts of the wicked. And take the helmet of salvation, and the sword of the Spirit, which is the word of God.**

This passage lists six pieces of armor: the loin belt, breastplate, shoes, shield, helmet, and sword. It seems as if the sword of the Spirit is where the list ends; however, there is one essential piece of weaponry missing from this list. We know this because ancient Roman armor always consisted of *seven* weapons, and Ephesians 6:13 says, "Wherefore take unto you the *whole armour* of God." Six pieces of weaponry is *not* the whole armor of God!

The Greek word for "whole armor" is *panoplia*. It is a compound of *pan*, meaning *all*, and *hoplon*, which is the Greek word for *weaponry*. Together it means *absolutely all the weaponry God has provided*. This word pictures *a soldier fully dressed in his armor from head to toe* and *a soldier's full attire and weaponry*. The following hardware was required in order for a soldier to be considered *fully dressed* for battle: the loin belt, breastplate, shoes, shield, helmet, sword, and lance. In Ephesians 6, Paul used the word *panoplia* to describe the physical weaponry God has given to every believer; therefore, we can conclude that there are also seven corresponding pieces of *spiritual* armor available to us.

The Roman *Pilum*

The loin belt worn by every Roman soldier held all of his armor together, and attached to it was a pouch that carried an array of lances or spears. Although we don't see the words "lance of intercession" in Ephesians 6:18, Paul did describe prayer in this way:

> **Praying always with all prayer and supplication in the Spirit, and watching thereunto with all perseverance and supplication for all saints.**

To provide more insight into Paul's description of prayer and the Roman soldier's lance, Rick read from his book, *Dressed To Kill*:

> When Paul came to the conclusion of this text about spiritual armor, he had the images of Roman lances and spears in his mind. It is quite possible that Paul was able to look over to the other side of his prison cell and see where his Roman guard had propped up against the wall several kinds of lances and spears of different sizes.
>
> The lances used by the large and diverse Roman army varied greatly in size, shape, and length. Over the course of many

centuries, these various lances had been modified substantially, so the Roman soldier had all kinds of lances at his disposal.

The old Greek lances…were about six to seven feet long with a solid iron lance-head at the end.

Some lances were small; others were extremely long. The smaller, shorter lances were used for gouging and thrusting at an enemy up close, whereas the longer lances were used for hurling at an enemy from a distance.

Most Roman soldiers carried both lances, short and long. With the shorter lance, they were able to thrust through the bodies of enemy soldiers at close range — and what a morbid death this was! With the longer lances, they would strike their adversary with a deadly blow from afar. After successfully hitting an enemy with this longer lance, the Roman soldier would draw his sword and run to finish off the opponent — cutting off his head while he lay wounded on the ground.

In addition to these, there were many other kinds of lances…. short lances, long lances, narrow lances, wide lances, pointed lances, dull lances, jagged lances, multiple-blade lances, and so forth. The average soldier in the infantry carried five short lances and one long lance.

Of all the lances in the ancient world, the Macedonians used the longest. The lance they used in battle was 21 to 24 feet long….

The Roman army used a lance called a *pilum*, which was primarily used for throwing at an enemy from a distance. These *pilum* lances were used when an opposing force came to attack the Romans' fortified position of encampment. Rather than wait for the enemy to come upon them before commencing the battle and thus take many losses, the Roman soldiers would hurl these extremely heavy lances through the air toward their foes. By doing this, the Romans could strike many of the enemy soldiers to the ground before they were able to penetrate their army encampment.

The length of the *pilum* by New Testament times was about six feet long…. Many of these lances have survived to this day and can be viewed in museums of antiquity around the world.

If the soldier desired to inflict a massive and terrible wound upon his enemy, he made sure to load his lance-head with extra iron. The heavier the instrument was, the more deadly was the wound. Furthermore, this heavier load of iron helped carry the lance farther when the soldier had to throw it a great distance.

There were many different kinds of lances and many variations of each one of them. In fact, there were so many shapes, sizes, and lengths of lances during that time in history that I could keep writing on this subject for many pages to come!

The Roman *pilum* was very heavy, and those carried by the Roman soldiers were very long. When not in use, the *pilum* could be pulled apart into smaller pieces like some fishing poles today. The Roman soldier would carry the pieces in his pouch on the backside of the loin belt. When needed for battle, it could quickly be pulled out of the pouch, assembled, and hurled at a distance against an approaching enemy.

All Kinds of Prayer

Ephesians 6:18 says, "Praying always with all prayer...." This phrase in Greek means *using all kinds of prayer*. One expositor has translated this as "using every kind of prayer that has been made available to use," which means there are multiple kinds of prayer.

We can find many different kinds of prayer in the Bible. There is the prayer of authority, the prayer of faith, the prayer of agreement, the prayer of intercession, the prayer of petition, and the prayer of supplication. And all of these types of prayer work differently.

There are various kinds of "lances" God has given to you that you are to keep in your pouch and ready to hurl at the enemy at any moment. When the enemy tries to launch an assault, don't wait for him to come close and get right in your face. Rather, early on and at the first sign of an attack, pull out the appropriate lance, hurl it, and hit the enemy from a distance!

When you discover that the enemy is coming with a big assault against you, load the lance head with extra weight as you begin to pray and intercede and hurl that weapon in the power of the Holy Spirit. No matter the situation, you can deal a deadly blow to the spiritual forces coming against you because there are all kinds of prayer that have been made available to you.

A Divine Toolbox

To illustrate this point further, Rick told a story on the program about his father's garage.

> My father loved his garage. He had so many tools! That's the trait of my father's that I didn't inherit. I'm not very mechanically inclined, and I'm not very good with tools. *But how my dad loved his tools!* Whenever I opened his toolbox, I would find a wrench, a flathead screwdriver, a Philips-head screwdriver, a hammer, and many other different tools. My father knew how to use each of those tools at the appropriate time and in the right way. He knew you couldn't use a hammer to screw in a screw; you couldn't use a screwdriver to hit a nail. You had to have the right tool for the right project. In the very same way, God has given to us all kinds of prayer; these are the spiritual lances made available to us.

The Lance Depends on the Loin Belt

In previous lessons we learned about the loin belt of the Roman soldier that the apostle Paul likened to the written Word of God — the Bible. On the loin belt there was attached a pouch that held the different lances used by the Roman soldier. In the same way a soldier's access to his lances depended on his loin belt being fixed in place, a believer's prayer life depends on the Word of God being a permanent, prioritized fixture in his life.

Very often our direction in prayer — what to pray, how to pray, the type of prayer to pray — will come to us as we are reading our Bible. Suddenly, the Holy Spirit will quicken a verse, and that verse gives us power in prayer. You'll find that many times you will be reading the wonderful Word of God and see exactly what you need to pray about a particular situation. It's as if the Holy Spirit has given you insight into the exact "lance" to hurl at the problem. Furthermore, He will often show you precisely how to load that lance head with extra weight to deal a deadly blow to the enemy.

When you become effective in prayer, you don't have to wait for the enemy to get up close. No, the moment you see trouble coming, you can head it off at the pass by hurling your lance of prayer. When you pray properly — according to the Word of God — you have much influence in the Spirit realm. The seventh and final weapon in the armor of God is not only a lance of intercession but a spear of influence!

STUDY QUESTIONS

> Study to shew thyself approved unto God, a workman that needeth
> not to be ashamed, rightly dividing the word of truth.
> — 2 Timothy 2:15

1. Explain when and how the *pilum* was used by the Roman soldier in battle.
2. What is the significance of lances coming in all shapes and sizes in comparison to prayer?
3. The Roman soldier always carried a pouch that held his various lances. Explain the importance of this pouch being connected to the loin belt as it relates to prayer.

PRACTICAL APPLICATION

> But be ye doers of the word, and not hearers only,
> deceiving your own selves.
> — James 1:22

1. Think of a time when you tried to fight a spiritual battle with natural weapons. What was the result and what did you learn?
2. Reflect on an instance when you used the spiritual weapons God has provided to overcome an attack of the enemy. What specifically did you do to overcome? What did you learn?
3. Before reading this lesson, had you ever heard of the "lance of prayer" being part of the armor of God? How has what you learned in this lesson impacted the way you will approach prayer going forward?

TOPIC

The Flesh Counts for Nothing

SCRIPTURES

1. **2 Corinthians 10:1-4** — Now I Paul myself beseech you by the meekness and gentleness of Christ, who in presence am base among you, but being absent am bold toward you: But I beseech you, that I may not be bold when I am present with that confidence, wherewith I think to be bold against some, which think of us as if we walked according to the flesh. For though we walk in the flesh, we do not war after the flesh: (For the weapons of our warfare are not carnal, but mighty through God to the pulling down of strong holds).

2. **Galatians 6:17** — From henceforth let no man trouble me: for I bear in my body the marks of the Lord Jesus.

3. **2 Corinthians 10:7** — Do ye look on things after the outward appearance…?

4. **2 Corinthians 10:10** — For his letters, say they, are weighty and powerful; but his bodily presence is weak, and his speech contemptible.

GREEK WORDS

1. "in presence" — **πρόσωπον** (*prosopon*): face, appearance, or countenance

2. "base" — **ταπεινός** (*tapeinos*): can picture something so shameful that it should not be put on public display; one who has become humble; to reduce one's self-importance; to make small; to minimize oneself; to be willing to stoop to any measure that is needed

3. "appearance" — **πρόσωπον** (*prosopon*): appearance, countenance, or face

4. "weighty" — **βαρύς** (*barus*): deep, deep, deep; heavy; profound

5. "powerful" — **ἰσχυρός** (*ischuros*): full of muscles; muscular; strong; mighty

6. "walk" — **περιπατέω** (*peripateo*): a compound of the words **περι** (*peri*) and **πατέω** (*pateo*); the word **περι** (*peri*) means around and suggests

the idea of something that is encircling; the word **πατέω** (*pateo*) means to walk and denotes the movement of the feet; when compounded, it means to habitually walk around in one general vicinity; to walk around in the flesh

7. "war" — **στρατεύομαι** (*strateuomai*): the activities of a committed, warring soldier; a strategic act of warfare; deciding a line of attack, what methods to use, including the approach that one charts in advance to conduct a well-thought-out assault

SYNOPSIS

Even though Paul was miles away from Corinth when he wrote his letters to the Corinthian church, he had gotten word about what the believers there had been saying about him. They were impressed by Paul's letters, but they didn't like the way he looked — they judged him according to the flesh.

The emphasis of this lesson:

The flesh counts for nothing. What truly counts is our stature in the spirit realm. We must learn to stop viewing ourselves and others according to the flesh and start seeing with the eyes of the Spirit. Who we are in Christ is what really counts.

Ephesians 6 tells of the whole armor of God. So far, we have covered all seven spiritual weapons: the loin belt, breastplate, shoes, shield, helmet, sword, and lance. Now that we understand why Paul likened each spiritual weapon to a particular corresponding physical weapon, let's dive into a new aspect of the weapons that have been made available to us.

Paul's Physical Appearance

Second Corinthians 10:1 says, "Now I, Paul myself beseech you by the meekness and gentleness of Christ, who in presence am base among you, but being absent am bold toward you." The first part of this verse seems complimentary. We would probably all like to be known for having the meekness and gentleness of Christ. But then Paul added, "…who in presence am base among you…."

The Greek word for "presence" is the word *prosopon* and literally means, *my face*. Paul was describing his *physical face*. The word "base" describes something so shameful it should not be put on public display. This is how

Paul described his physical appearance. We know Paul had been through multiple persecutions and had been beaten repeatedly. It seems that as a result of those beatings, there was something physically wrong with his face.

In Galatians 6:17, Paul stated, "I bear in my body the marks of the Lord Jesus." It is likely that in addition to Paul's body being beaten, his face had also been affected by the lashes that had struck various parts of his body.

The Greek word for the phrase "who in presence" in Second Corinthians 10:1 is the word *prosopon* and means Paul was essentially saying, "…according to my face am base; my face is so shameful it should not be on public display."

In this passage, Paul was simply describing what others had been saying about him. Apparently, the Corinthians were saying, things like, "You know, Paul has good character; he has the meekness and gentleness of Christ. But his face…if only we didn't have to look at his face!"

Paul's Weighty Letters

Paul continued his letter to the Corinthians in verse 7: "Do ye look on things after the outward appearance…?" In Greek, the words "outward appearance" are from the same word translated "presence" in verse 1, which is *prosopon*. Paul was saying, "You're looking at my face."

In verse 10, Paul quoted the private conversations of those who had been criticizing him. Even though Paul was miles and miles away from Corinth, God gave him insight into what the Corinthians had been saying about him. This is a lesson to believers to be careful about what we say behind closed doors about our pastor or a preacher. We may think they will never know what we have been saying, but God has a way of making sure people know what you are saying about them!

The Corinthians had been saying, "For his letters, say they, are weighty and powerful… (2 Corinthians 10:10). The word "weighty" is from the Greek word *barus*, which describes *that which is deep*. The word "powerful" is a form of the Greek word *ischuros*, which describes *muscles*. When you put it all together, it is the equivalent of saying, "Wow! Paul can really write a letter! His letters are deep; they are profound; they will really give you spiritual muscles. But his bodily presence is weak; his face is weak; and his speech is contemptible." It is as if they were saying to him, "Paul, we love your letters. Nobody can write a letter better than you. Your letters are deep, and they are so muscular. But your face is so hard to look at. Could you just write us a letter and stay home? We really don't want to look at you."

The Flesh Counts for Nothing

We can see in the Scriptures that one of the big problems for the people of the Corinthian church was that they were very affected by fleshly things. They were a flesh-dominated church. The Corinthian church has been described as the Las Vegas of the First Century. They liked style and fashion, and they liked very beautiful, expensive, presentable things. So when Paul stood before them, they didn't want to look at his face, and they judged him according to his physical appearance.

On the program, Rick told a story about an experience he had with a particular church pastor many years ago:

> As Denise and I were traveling and ministering in the northwestern part of the United States, I began to get calls from a pastor on the East Coast. This pastor was hounding me, saying things like, "I need you to come to my church." A few days would pass, and he would call again, saying, "I need you to come to my church." He kept imploring me, "Please, I need you to come. I need you to do several meetings in my church." A few more days would pass, and he would call again.

> Finally, I asked him, "Why is it so urgent that I come to your church?" He responded, "I've got to tell you the truth, brother Rick, I haven't been saved very long, and I don't know the Bible very well. I've gotten all your series and have been preaching them almost verbatim in my church, and I'm almost out of your series. I don't know what I'm going to preach; I have nothing else to listen to. I need you to come to my church because I'm running out of material!"

> I was really amazed, especially when I heard that about 900 people were already attending his church. This was a lot of people attending the church for a pastor who had only been saved a couple of years. Denise and I finally surrendered and told him we would come.

> When we arrived, because I wanted to know why this church was growing so quickly, I decided to go to the church as a visitor and

ask to meet the pastor. I wanted to see what I could figure out about this church before I announced who I was.

I walked in and said to the greeter, "I would like to meet the pastor. This is my first time here." The greeter looked at me and literally said, "Our pastor doesn't really have time for people like you, he's waiting on a special guest."

Well, I found that very interesting, so I just wandered around. I looked at the auditorium, I saw that the rows were filling up with churchgoers, and people were getting ready for service. There was a great expectation.

Finally, I went back to that same greeter, and I said, "Would you just please ask the pastor if he would allow me to meet him? It's my first time here." The greeter said to me, "You're just kind of a problem, aren't you?" He didn't know who he was talking to.

He finally said, "All right, I'm going to ask the pastor." So he knocked on the pastor's door, and said, "Pastor, there's a man out here who just insists on meeting you." The pastor said, "Well, let's bring him on in."

I walked in, and when I saw the pastor, I could hardly believe my eyes. He was sitting behind the desk in a very high-backed chair, and all the lights in his room were focused on the desk, so he was very well lighted.

He had long, long, long silver hair that flipped up on the end, kind of like my sister would have worn her hair back in the 1960s. He had a big, gold chain wrapped around his neck, and on the end of the gold chain there was a big eagle that was encrusted with rubies and diamonds. On each of his fingers, he wore diamond-encrusted jewelry, and on his wrists were big bracelets. I was pretty shocked by what I saw.

I walked across the room, reached across the desk to shake his hand, and said, "Pastor, my name is Rick Renner, it is such a privilege to meet you."

Well, how do you think he responded? He looked at me, kind of leaned back, pushed back from his desk, and stood up and asked, "Where were you the last time we talked on the phone?"

He didn't believe I was Rick Renner! He was checking me out to see if I was really who I said I was. I told him where I had been the last time we spoke, and he responded "Oh, well, you really are Rick Renner. You're a little different from what I anticipated."

Back in those days, there weren't many visuals that someone could watch, so this pastor had been listening to my cassette tapes. As he listened, he had in his mind an imagination of what I would look like. He probably thought I would look like him; that I'd be draped in gold and have long hair and a bouffant hairdo.

Instead, in walked Rick Renner, who is just about as ordinary as anybody and balding — nothing spectacular. I did *not* meet his expectation; he was judging me according to the flesh.

There's nothing wrong with my physical appearance; I'm fine with who I am. I started losing my hair when I was 17 years old. I wouldn't even know what to do if I had hair. As a matter of fact, I don't even want hair! But I knew he was judging me according to the flesh.

As I stood there in front of him, I thought to myself, *Buddy, you're going to find out this week that I do not war according to the flesh. You're judging me according to the flesh, but you're going to see what the Spirit of God does through me in these meetings.*

He would learn that the flesh counts for nothing.

The Committed Warring Soldier

Of course, we should dress up our flesh, eat right, exercise, and look the best that we can. But when it comes to spiritual things, we cannot produce them by the flesh. This is exactly what Paul was saying in Second Corinthians 10:1-3:

> **Now I Paul myself beseech you by the meekness and gentleness of Christ, who in presence** [according to my face] **am base among you** [I should not be on public display among you], **but being absent am bold toward you: But I beseech you, that I may not be bold when I am present with that confidence, wherewith I think to be bold against some, which think of us as if we walked according to the flesh. For though we walk in the flesh, we do not war after the flesh.**

Notice, verse 3 says, "For though we walk…." The Greek word for "walk" is *peripateo*. The word *peri* means *around* and the word *pateo* means *to walk* and could be translated, "though we walk around in the flesh."

You live in a human body, and most of what you do is in the flesh. You talk in the flesh, you reproduce in the flesh, you sleep in the flesh, you eat in the flesh. You cannot get away from your body. Even at this very moment, you are in the flesh.

But Paul says, "…we do not *war* after the flesh." The word "war" is the Greek word *strateuomai*, which describes the activities of a committed, warring soldier. Paul was describing who he was in the *Spirit*. Even though in the natural realm Paul may have been a small guy with a face that others thought was not presentable, he said, "Wait until you see who I am in the spirit world, because in that dimension, I am like a soldier that is well skilled and well trained. I can defeat the enemy because I do not war according to the flesh."

Friend, it is the same for you. Your flesh counts for nothing when it comes to the weight you carry in the Spirit. Don't make the same mistake the Corinthians did; they viewed Paul after the flesh, and they grossly misjudged who Paul really was and what he could do in the Spirit. Remember, it's not about what you look like on the outside, but it is about the Holy Spirit in you and who you are on the inside.

STUDY QUESTIONS

Study to shew thyself approved unto God, a workman that needeth not to be ashamed, rightly dividing the word of truth.
— 2 Timothy 2:15

1. What were the Corinthians saying about Paul's personal appearance and how did this compare to Paul's character?
2. What is the meaning behind the word "weighty" in Second Corinthians 10:10, and how does this relate to Paul's letters?
3. Describe who Paul was in the spirit realm according to the Greek word *strateuomai* found in Second Corinthians 10:3.

PRACTICAL APPLICATION

> But be ye doers of the word, and not hearers only,
> deceiving your own selves.
> —James 1:22

1. First Samuel 16:7 says, "…For the Lord seeth not as man seeth; for man looketh on the outward appearance, but the Lord looketh on the heart." Describe a time when you were wrongly judged by someone because that person only considered your outward appearance. Did you have an understanding of who you were in Christ? How did it feel to be misjudged?

2. Have you ever similarly misjudged someone? What happened? How did you handle the situation once you realized your mistake? What was the outcome?

3. Read Acts 10:9-48. Explain verses 28 and 29, which says, "…God hath shewed me that I should not call any man common or unclean. Therefore came I unto you without gainsaying, as soon as I was sent for." How would Paul have previously judged Cornelius and the other Gentiles? Why is it important not to be judgmental toward those we encounter in this life?

LESSON 18

TOPIC

Weapons Are Mighty Through God

SCRIPTURES

1. **2 Corinthians 10:1** — Now I Paul myself beseech you by the meekness and gentleness of Christ, who in presence am base among you, but being absent am bold toward you.

2. **2 Corinthians 10:7** — Do ye look on things after the outward appearance…?

3. **2 Corinthians 10:10** — For his letters, say they, are weighty and powerful; but his bodily presence is weak, and his speech contemptible.

4. **Galatians 6:17** — ...for I bear in my body the marks of the Lord Jesus.

5. **2 Corinthians 10:2,3** — But I beseech you, that I may not be bold when I am present with that confidence, wherewith I think to be bold against some, which think of us as if we walked according to the flesh. For though we walk in the flesh, we do not war after the flesh.

6. **Luke 4:33,34** — And in the synagogue there was a man, which had a spirit of an unclean devil, and cried out with a loud voice, saying, Let us alone; what have we to do with thee, thou Jesus of Nazareth? art thou come to destroy us? I know thee who thou art; the Holy One of God.

7. **2 Corinthians 10:3,4** — For though we walk in the flesh, we do not war after the flesh: (For the weapons of our warfare are not carnal, but mighty through God to the pulling down of strong holds).

8. **Joshua 6:20** — So the people shouted when the priests blew with the trumpets: and it came to pass, when the people heard the sound of the trumpet, and the people shouted with a great shout, that the wall fell down flat, so that the people went up into the city, every man straight before him, and they took the city.

GREEK WORDS

1. "in presence" — **πρόσωπον** (*prosopon*): face, appearance, or countenance

2. "base" — **ταπεινός** (*tapeinos*): can picture something so shameful that it should not be put on public display; one who has become humble; to reduce one's self-importance; to make small; to minimize oneself; to be willing to stoop to any measure that is needed

3. "outward appearance" — **πρόσωπον** (*prosopon*): face, appearance, or countenance

4. "war" — **στρατεύομαι** (*strateuomai*): the activities of a committed, warring soldier; a strategic act of warfare; deciding a line of attack, what methods to use, including the approach that one charts in advance to conduct a well-thought-out assault

5. "weapons" — **ὅπλα** (*hopla*) the full weaponry of a Roman soldier; weapons

6. "warfare" — **στρατεία** (*strateia*): the word for a well-planned, strategic attack; a campaign; depicts strategic warfare; includes a line of attack,

methods to be used in an attack, and the route chosen to carry out a debilitating assault; where we get the word strategy

7. "mighty" — δυνατός (*dunatos*): from the word ύναμις (dunamis), meaning powerful might; explosive power; a force of nature, like an earthquake, tornado, or hurricane; the full might of the advancing Roman army; where we get the word "dynamite"; ability; power; amazing ability; to be able, capable, or competent for any task; a force that causes one to be able or capable; competent

8. "strong holds" — ὀχύρωμα (*ochuroma*): well-defended lie; a fortress; castle; citadel; pictures a stronghold with walls fortified to keep outsiders on the outside; a dreadful prison constructed deep inside a fortress that was intended to prevent a hostage or prisoner from escaping; a place of arrest, captivity, confinement, detention, imprisonment, or incarceration

9. "pulling down" — καθαιρέω (*kathaireo*): to demolish; to destroy; to dismantle; to throw down; to knock down, break up, pull apart, and take to pieces, until nothing is left standing; to disassemble, if needed, bit by bit; used to picture pulling down the walls of a well-defended fortress

SYNOPSIS

The church of Corinth was made up of people who were very flesh-minded and who didn't like Paul's physical appearance. What they didn't realize was that Paul's appearance in the Spirit was like that of a fully trained, highly skilled Roman soldier. All of hell knew Paul's name!

The emphasis of this lesson:

Because we live in a natural world, we all walk in our physical bodies, or the flesh, daily. We talk, sleep, and think in the flesh — but we should never judge others according to the flesh. As believers, our identity in Christ is what really counts; who we are in the Spirit will cause the kingdom of darkness to tremble because the spiritual weapons we carry are mighty through God.

Don't Judge According to the Flesh

In the previous lesson, we learned about one reason the apostle Paul wrote to the Corinthian church. Paul found out that the people had been judging him according to his outward appearance. He began chapter 10 of Second Corinthians with a compliment, then followed it with a rebuke:

Now I, Paul, myself beseech you by the meekness and gentleness of Christ, who in presence am base among you, but being absent am bold toward you.

— 2 Corinthians 10:1

The word "presence" is the Greek word *prosopon* and means *the face*. The word "base" describes *something so shameful that it should not be put on public display*. Paul essentially said, "I beseech you by the meekness and gentleness of Christ. That's good, but my face is so shameful that some of you are alleging it shouldn't be put on public display."

Because the people at the church of Corinth were very flesh-dominated and greatly affected by outward things, Paul had to address the issue. He referred to this again in Second Corinthians 10:7.

Do you look on things after the outward appearance?

The words "outward appearance" are translated from the same Greek word *prosopon*, which means *the face*. Second Corinthians 10:7 could be translated, "You're looking at me and judging me according to my face."

Not only were the Corinthians judging Paul by his face, but they were also judging his physical appearance in general. In verse 10, Paul wrote about what the Corinthians had been saying about his physical body:

For his letters, say they, are weighty and powerful, but his bodily presence is weak, and his speech is contemptible.

Paul found out what the Corinthians had been saying about him. It was as if they were saying, "We love your letters, Paul. Your letters are so meaty and very deep. We know that if we obey your letters, they'll put muscles on us. But your body is just so despicable, and your speech so contemptable. Why don't you just stay home and write us letters? We really don't want to look at you."

So the question arises, what was so wrong with Paul's face and his body? We know that during the course of Paul's ministry, he had been beaten over and over again. In fact, in Galatians 6:17, Paul wrote "…I bear in my body the marks of the Lord Jesus." Paul literally bore the marks from all of the beatings he received, and it is possible that the straps he was beaten with also affected his face.

In verse 2 of Second Corinthians 10, Paul wrote:

> **But I beseech you that I may not be bold when I'm present with that confidence, wherewith I think to be bold against some which think of us as if we walked according to the flesh.**

Paul essentially said, "I hear what you're saying about me, and I'm thinking about showing you just how bold this flesh can be."

Paul continued in verse 3: "For though we walk in the flesh, we do not war after the flesh." The truth is that to some degree, we all walk in the flesh and are living in the flesh. Even if we don't like our body, we are living in it. We walk, talk, sleep, and think in the flesh. And the reality is, we cannot fully escape our flesh until we pass from this life into the next.

But there is good news found in verse 3:

> **For though we walk in the flesh, we do not war after the flesh.**

The word "war" is translated from the Greek word that describes *the attitude and actions of a fully committed Roman soldier*. Paul was comparing himself to a Roman soldier — a trained killer! In the spirit realm, Paul was so mighty that a demon-possessed man said, "Jesus I know, and Paul I know," (Acts 19:15). Hell literally knew Paul's name! *WOW!*

A Holy Terror to the Kingdom of Darkness

On the program, Rick told the following story:

> Many years ago, in the middle of the night, as I sat in the ferry station on Staten Island, New York City, I saw a man dragging himself along the ground. The man appeared to be homeless, and as he dragged himself across the floor from the opposite side of the station, he headed straight to me.

> The man finally got up on his feet, looked at me and said, "I know who you are, and this town isn't big enough for both of us!" This man was demonized, and the demon in him recognized who I was in the spirit; he saw that I was a spiritual warrior!

This experience reminded me of the time when Jesus went home to Nazareth after He was baptized in the Holy Spirit. Jesus had grown up in Nazareth, yet during the first 30 years of His life, there was never a demonic manifestation. But when Jesus was baptized in the Holy Spirit at the River Jordan, He was dressed in the whole weaponry of God; He changed in the spirit realm. When He arrived back home, He walked down the same streets He had always walked, but now there was a different response.

Demon-possessed people began screaming, "I know who you are, the Holy One of God!" (*See* Luke 4:34.) Jesus was dressed the same, His hair was the same, His physical appearance hadn't changed. Externally, everything remained the same, but when Jesus was baptized in the Holy Spirit, He was dressed in the whole armor of God. In the spirit realm, the demons could see that Jesus was a mighty warrior.

That night in the Staten Island ferry station, the demonized man wasn't moved by what I was wearing. He was moved by what he saw in the spirit realm. And in that realm, he saw me as a mighty warrior.

I had a second experience on the streets of San Francisco. I was with my mother, who was a Southern Baptist. As we were walking down the street, in front of us was a man who looked very dirty. He was cursing and foul. He was walking in the same direction as us, but he didn't see us behind him.

Suddenly, as my mother and I were walking, he turned around, looked directly at me, and said, "I know who you are." You would have thought that this man had eyes in the back of his head. He had been looking forward, yet, spiritually, he knew who was behind him.

He then turned around and began spitting. Of course, I took authority over this in the name of Jesus, but he knew who I was in the Spirit realm. just like that demon knew Paul's name. One of the greatest compliments I've ever received is that hell knows my name!

When we are dressed in the whole armor of God, we become a holy terror to the kingdom of darkness. That is who we are in the spirit realm when we are dressed in the whole armor of God. When we are clothed with all of the weaponry God has made available to us, the kingdom of darkness trembles!

A Divine Strategy

Second Corinthians 10:3 and 4 says,

For though we walk in the flesh, we do not war after the flesh: (for the weapons of our warfare are not carnal, but mighty through God to the pulling down of strongholds).

The word "weapons" is from the Greek word *hopla*. The plural form is used in this instance and describes *the full weaponry of a Roman soldier*. Figuratively, that is what Paul was describing in this passage. As we have studied from Ephesians 6, God has given us seven pieces of weaponry to repel the attacks of the enemy.

In Second Corinthians 10:3 and 4, the word "warfare" is from the Greek word *strateia*, which describes *a well-planned, strategic attack*. It is derived from a Greek word that depicts *strategic warfare, including a line of attack, the methods to be used in the debilitating attack, and the route chosen to implement it*.

Not only has God given us spiritual weapons to attack the enemy, but He has also given us a strategy for *how* to attack the enemy. It is not enough to have weapons alone; we must have a well-defined strategy. That is what the Holy Spirit can give us. God will always give us a strategy.

In Joshua 6, when God spoke to the children of Israel and instructed them to take the city of Jericho, they did the unthinkable according to the flesh. They walked around the city of Jericho one time each day for six days and on the seventh day, they walked around its walls seven times. It all seemed so foolish according to the flesh, but on that seventh time around the city, they raised their voices, the walls came tumbling down, and God gave them the city!

The children of Israel implemented the strategy God had given them. If you are dealing with some kind of an attack, God has already given you weapons to deal with it. But He also has a divine strategy to give you.

Divinely Empowered Weapons

Again, verse 4 of Second Corinthians 10 says:

> **…For the weapons of our warfare are not carnal but mighty through God to the pulling down of strongholds**

The word "mighty," is the Greek word *dynata*, and it is a form of the word *dunamis*, which describes *powerful might*. It is the same Greek word used to describe *a force of nature like an earthquake, tornado, or hurricane*. This is the kind of power released through us when we are operating with our spiritual weapons. One translation says that our weapons are "divinely empowered."

The word "stronghold" in Second Corinthians 10:4 describes *a well-defended lie or fortress*. Many people have been taken captive by mental strongholds, but just because they are dealing with a stronghold doesn't mean they have to live with it. The words "pulling down" mean *to demolish, destroy, dismantle, throw down, knock down, break up, break apart and pull to pieces until nothing is left*.

Rick shared in a previous lesson that when he was young, his father needed some bricks to build a new garage. Rather than buy new bricks, he bought an old house in downtown Tulsa, Oklahoma, that needed to be torn down. Every evening, Rick and his father would begin to dismantle the walls, brick by brick. They would use hammers to knock the old mortar off the bricks until the bricks were clean and the house was totally dismantled.

We must be fully committed to using the power of God and our divinely empowered weapons to dismantle the strongholds in our life — brick by brick, if necessary. We must be determined to knock strongholds down and completely dismantle them until we are free of what has been controlling us.

STUDY QUESTIONS

> **Study to shew thyself approved unto God, a workman that needeth not to be ashamed, rightly dividing the word of truth.**
> **— 2 Timothy 2:15**

1. In your own words, explain the meaning behind Paul's words found in Second Corinthians 10:3 and 4, which says, "For though we walk in the flesh, we do not war after the flesh: (For the weapons of our warfare are not carnal, but mighty through God to the pulling down of strong holds)." Why is it important for believers to understand the meaning of this passage?

2. Acts 19 tells the story of the seven sons of Sceva who were challenged by an evil spirit. Verse 15 says the spirit said to them, "Jesus I know, and Paul I know, but who are ye?" Explain the significance of the evil spirit's comment regarding Paul.

PRACTICAL APPLICATION

> But be ye doers of the word, and not hearers only,
> deceiving your own selves.
> — James 1:22

1. Read Joshua 6. Have you ever received a divine strategy from God that seemed silly to your natural mind? Did you heed the Holy Spirit's instructions? What was the result?

2. When we are dressed in the whole armor of God, we become a holy terror to the kingdom of darkness. Consider your daily life. Are you living every day dressed in the whole armor of God? What adjustments will you make to ensure you are walking in the fullness of your identity in Christ? Cause the kingdom of darkness to tremble!

LESSON 19

TOPIC

How To Cast Down Imaginations

SCRIPTURES

1. **2 Corinthians 10:4-6** — For the weapons of our warfare are not carnal, but mighty through God to the pulling down of strong holds; casting down imaginations, and every high thing that exalteth itself against the knowledge of God, and bringing into captivity every

thought to the obedience of Christ; and having in readiness to revenge all disobedience, when your obedience is fulfilled.

2. **John 8:36** — If the Son therefore shall make you free, ye shall be free indeed

3. **Ephesians 6:13** — Wherefore take unto you the whole armour of God

GREEK WORDS

1. "weapons" — **ὅπλα** (*hopla*): the full weaponry of a Roman soldier; weapons

2. "warfare" — **στρατεία** (*strateia*) where we get the word strategy; a line of attack, the way to attack, when to attack; the word for a well-planned, strategic attack; a campaign; depicts strategic warfare; includes a line of attack, methods to be used in an attack, and the route chosen to carry out a debilitating assault

3. "carnal" — **σαρκός** (*sarkos*): fleshly; carnal nature; base fleshly instincts

4. "mighty" — **δυνατός** (dunatos): terrifically powerful; from the word **ύναμις** (dunamis): powerful might; explosive power; a force of nature, like an earthquake, tornado, or hurricane; the full might of the advancing Roman army; where we get the word "dynamite"; ability; power; amazing ability; to be able, capable, or competent for any task; a force that causes one to be able or capable; competent

5. "pulling down" — **καθαιρέω** (kathaireo): to demolish; to destroy; to dismantle; to throw down; to knock down, break up, pull apart, and take to pieces, until nothing is left standing; to disassemble, if needed, bit by bit; used to picture pulling down the walls of a well-defended fortress

6. "strong holds" — **ὀχύρωμα** (*ochuroma*): castle; prison; pictures a stronghold with walls fortified to keep outsiders on the outside; a dreadful prison constructed deep inside a fortress that was intended to prevent a hostage or prisoner from escaping; a place of arrest, captivity, confinement, detention, imprisonment, or incarceration

7. "casting down" — **καθαιρέω** (*kathaireo*): to demolish; to destroy; to dismantle; to throw down; to knock down, break up, pull apart, and take to pieces, until nothing is left standing; to disassemble, if needed, bit by bit; used to picture pulling down the walls of a well-defended fortress

8. "imaginations" — λογισμός (*logismos*): imaginations; reasonings; where we get the word logic, as in logical thinking; used to denote thoughts or reasoning in the mind

9. "bringing into captivity" — αἰχμαλωτίζω (*aichmalotidzo*): the spear of a Roman soldier; to take captive at a spear point; to take captive as a prisoner; to put the spear into the back of a captive and forcibly drive him into captivity; manipulation by physical force or by mental or spiritual suggestion

SYNOPSIS

Second Corinthians 10:4 tells us that our spiritual weapons are for pulling down strongholds. But what is a stronghold? According to the apostle Paul's description, strongholds are a demonic strategy meant to enslave a person so deeply that he or she is completely incapacitated and ineffective in the kingdom of God.

The emphasis of this lesson:

The captive enemy of a Roman soldier was always at the mercy of the soldier's spear. If a soldier pressed his spearhead into the back of his enemy, that prisoner would be forced to obey. Just as the Roman soldier's spearhead caused his captive to go wherever the soldier desired him to go, we must put a spiritual spearhead in the back of any thought that attempts to infiltrate our mind.

Spiritual Armor and a Divine Strategy

In previous lessons we learned that the list of spiritual weapons the apostle Paul described in Ephesians 6 is available to every believer. Ephesians 6:13 says, "Wherefore take unto you the *whole armour* of God, that ye may be able to withstand in the evil day, and having done all, to stand." The Greek word for "whole armor" is *panoplia*. It is a compound of *pan*, meaning *all*, and *hoplon*, which is the Greek word for *weaponry*. Second Corinthians 10:4 says, "For the weapons of our warfare are not carnal…" and the word "weapons" here is the same word *haplon*, which describes *the full weaponry of the Roman soldier*.

When we are filled with the Holy Spirit and walk in the power of God, that power dresses us in all of the weaponry available to us. That is the reason it is vital that we don't step away from the power of God. When we choose to step away from His power, the weaponry begins to fall off. But as long as the power of God is operating in us, we are walking in the *whole armor* of God.

Again, Second Corinthians 10:4 says, "For the weapons of our *warfare....*" The word "warfare" is the Greek word *strateia* and is we derive our English word "strategy." It does not describe warfare alone but the *way* to attack and *when* to attack.

Not only does God grace us with every weapon we need, if we will listen to the Holy Spirit, He will also give us a divine strategy for when to act and when to be silent; when to move and when to be still; and how to attack and what avenue to use. The Holy Spirit will show us exactly what to do. We must battle in cooperation with the Holy Spirit. This means we must have ears to hear what the Spirit is speaking to us.

Every Roman soldier needed more than weaponry; he also needed wisdom about how to use his weapons. He needed to know when to be quiet and when to act. God, in His goodness, not only gives us powerful weapons, but He also gives us a divine strategy for how to use them.

Second Corinthians 10:4 continues, "For the weapons of our warfare are not *carnal...*" The word "carnal" is the Greek word *sarkos*, which means *fleshly*. When Paul states that our weapons are "not carnal," he means those weapons are *not fleshly*. The mind will not produce these weapons. They cannot be produced with human effort or talent. These weapons and their use occur in the unseen spirit realm by the direction of the Holy Spirit.

Demolishing Strongholds

Paul continued in Second Corinthians 10:4 by describing the weapons of our warfare and letting us know what they are for:

> **For the weapons of our warfare are not carnal, but *mighty* through God to the *pulling down* of strong holds.**

The word "mighty" used in this verse is a form of the Greek word *dunatos* and describes something that is *terrifically powerful* through God. One translation says these weapons are "divinely empowered" to the pulling down of strongholds. The Greek meaning for the phrase "pulling down" creates a vivid picture. It means *to demolish, to destroy, to dismantle, to throw down, to knock down, to break up, to break apart,* and *to pull the pieces until nothing is left.*

In a previous lesson, Rick told the story of when his father needed bricks to build a new garage. Rather than purchasing brand new bricks, he bought an old, abandoned house in downtown Tulsa, Oklahoma, that needed to be demolished. He said to Rick, "You and I are going down to that site every day when I get off work, and we're going to take that old brick house apart, piece by piece."

Rick and his father drove to the house the first day, and his father said, "We will not be finished until we have completely dismantled this house." Because Rick was young, he thought, *You have got to be kidding me. We're going to take this house apart brick by brick?!*

But Rick's father showed him exactly how they would accomplish this. As Rick watched, his father knocked out the first brick, but before he moved on to the next one, he cleaned off the brick by knocking off all the mortar until it was completely mortar-free. After that, he put that clean brick in a nice, neat place and moved on to the next brick. He then invited Rick to join him, and together they began to dismantle that house until, finally, it was in pieces.

However, this project was not completed in one day; it wasn't even done after one week. It took Rick and his father more than a whole month of traveling to and from the abandoned house and pulling it apart brick by brick.

Some people get discouraged in their attempts to pull down strong holds in their own lives because the first attempt isn't completely successful. But this is the reason we must be fully committed and refuse to stop until we are totally free. Even if we have to do it one piece at a time, we must be determined to continue until the strong hold is completely dismantled and removed from our life.

Strongholds

Second Corinthians 10:4 says that our weapons are for pulling down strongholds. But what is a stronghold? To give additional insight into the definition of a strong hold, Rick read from his study guide called *Healing the Mind and Emotions of the Oppressed*:

> The Greek word for "stronghold" is *ochuroma*, which literally describes a castle or fortress with walls fortified to keep an outsider on the outside. The same word describes a dreadful prison

constructed deep inside a fortress intended to prevent a hostage or prisoner from escaping. It is a place of arrest, captivity, confinement, detention, imprisonment, or incarceration. When you have a mental stronghold, it is like a castle has been built in your brain. The devil, like a wicked king, moves into the castle. From this high place in your life, from your mind and your emotions, he begins dictating to you, subduing you, telling you what to believe, what to feel, and what will happen to you. He builds that fortress so securely in your mind and emotions, it traps you like you are in a prison. Even worse, others who try to help you cannot seem to penetrate because the walls of the lie are so thick that when they tell you the truth, you cannot hear them. The truth cannot penetrate because you have been insulated by a lie.

A person living with a mental stronghold is living as if he or she is trapped inside a prison with imaginary bars. The imprisonment is not real, but it seems very real to the prisoner within that stronghold. This person may feel very limited or less valuable than others when, in fact, he or she is very talented or even more gifted than others. The devil has enslaved this person in a lie.

Second Corinthians 10:5 says, "Casting down imaginations, and every high thing that exalteth itself against the knowledge of God, and bringing into captivity every thought to the obedience of Christ." The Greek word for "casting down" is the very same Greek word used in verse 4 for "pulling down," which means *to demolish, to destroy, to dismantle, to throw down, to knock down, to break up, to break apart*, and *to pull the pieces until nothing is left*. The word "imaginations" is the Greek word *logismos*, which can be translated *imaginations* or *reasonings*.

According to the apostle Paul's description, strongholds take place in the mind of a person. Strongholds are imaginary, and they are lies from the devil meant to enslave a person so deeply that he or she is completely incapacitated and ineffective.

Two Types of Strongholds

There are two kinds of strongholds: *illogical* strongholds and *logical* strongholds.

Illogical Strongholds

An example of an *illogical* stronghold is a person who is thin but sees himself as overweight. He becomes enslaved to the idea that he is fat. This is the reason people become anorexic. They are living according to a lie that is dictating to them that they are fat when, in fact, they are actually too thin. Yet, to those living with this illogical stronghold, this lie seems completely true.

Another example is when a person who is greatly talented, believes the lie that he or she is not talented or is less gifted than others or not gifted at all. This is false. It is an *illogical* stronghold.

Logical Strongholds

A *logical* stronghold seems to make sense to our reasoning. For example, someone might be feeling as though God is telling him to leave his job and move to another country. But because he just got a promotion and is making good money, he decides that he can't do what God is telling him to do and becomes enslaved to the logic of his reasoning, never stepping out in faith. As a result, he never experiences the adventure that is God's will for his life.

The *logical* strongholds can be just as difficult to defeat as *illogical* strongholds because the *logical* strongholds make sense. But regardless of what type of stronghold a person is dealing with, he must be committed to cast it down. He must be willing to say, "I *will* walk free of this lie. I refuse to live in this illusion any longer, and I will not be dominated by these false perceptions of myself. I will dismantle this lie piece by piece, if necessary, until it is completely demolished."

Casting Down Imaginations

Second Corinthians 10:5 says, "Casting down imaginations, and every high thing that exalteth itself against the knowledge of God, and bringing into captivity every thought to the obedience of Christ." The "knowledge of God" is simply what the Bible says about us. The Bible says we are healed and righteous and that we have peace of mind. But the devil doesn't want us to walk in any of those benefits of being a child of God.

Although the Bible says that you are healed, the enemy will try to exalt himself and the symptoms in your body against what God says in His Word. He will say, "You're sick. You've always been sick. You're always going to be sick. You're never going to be set free of this sickness." His goal is to enslave your mind with that wrong belief, exalting itself above the Word of God.

Although the Bible says that you are righteous the enemy will try to exalt himself and his lies by saying, "You're unrighteous. You're unworthy. You're nothing." He is trying to exalt those negative thoughts about you over you until a strong hold is formed and you are dominated by it.

Although the Bible says that the peace of God belongs to you, the enemy will try to exalt himself in your mind by saying, "I'm going to keep your life and emotions in turmoil." If you don't resist him and use your spiritual weaponry to pull down these strong holds, you will become enslaved to the lies of the enemy and never fully walk in the will of God for your life.

There are always two voices speaking to us at all times. The voice of God is always speaking, telling us who we are and what we possess because of Jesus' sacrifice on the Cross. There is also the voice of the enemy that is working to steal, kill, and destroy everything the Word of God says belongs to us. We must decide which voice we will heed. The voice we listen to will determine whether we live in a state of freedom in Christ or a state of bondage to the devil's lies. We must close our ears to the lies and inundate our mind with the Word of God.

As we fill and bombard our minds with the Word of God, we will break those lying "bricks" apart until our minds are completely free. God has given us divinely empowered weapons that enable us to war against and defeat the false imaginations from the enemy, but we must use the weapons and not give up!

The Head of the Spear

You may be wondering, *How do I pull down strong holds?* The apostle Paul let us know the answer to this question in Second Corinthians 10:5:

> **Casting down imaginations, and every high thing that exalteth itself against the knowledge of God, and bringing into captivity every thought to the obedience of Christ.**

The Greek phrase "bringing into captivity" describes the spear of a Roman soldier. If a soldier pressed his spearhead into the back of his enemy, that enemy would be forced to obey. The soldier controlled the direction his captive enemy would go because his spearhead gave him the advantage over his enemy. Because the enemy knew his life was on the line, if the Roman soldier said, "Turn left," the enemy would obey. If the soldier said, "Turn right," the enemy would acquiesce. The prisoner was very aware there was the tip of a spear in his back, which meant the Roman soldier could force the captive to go any direction he desired.

This is the picture Paul was painting when he told us to "take into captivity every thought." Instead of being controlled by any thought that enters our mind, we must put the tip of the spear into the back of that negative thought and tell our mind what we will and will not allow it to think. With the Word of God, we can put the tip of the spear into our mind and direct our thoughts.

Rather than listening to every thought that comes to mind, start speaking the Word of God to every thought that comes to mind. You do not have to accept every thought that tries to infiltrate your thinking. You can do what Second Corinthians 10:5 says and take captive *every thought*.

The Renewed Mind

Remember, the process of pulling down a mental stronghold — whether logical or illogical — is going to take time and will require your dedication. Second Corinthians 10:6 says, "And having in a readiness to revenge all disobedience, when your obedience is fulfilled." This means you must be committed to use everything you have to revenge every disobedient thought until, finally, your mind is in your control and renewed by the Word of God.

This is why we must understand the spiritual weapons God has given us and that these weapons must be used with a divine strategy. If we use the weapons God has given us and receive a strategy from the Holy Ghost, we will be able to pull down every lying imagination in our mind.

It all comes down to this: What you hear is what you will believe and what you believe will become your reality. Learning to listen to the truth of God's Word and speaking it against the lies of the enemy will demolish falsehoods. You can step into everything that the Word of God says you are. You can experience your healing; you can experience the peace God! But you must be determined to pull down any stronghold in your mind that exalts itself over the knowledge of God.

STUDY QUESTIONS

> Study to shew thyself approved unto God, a workman that needeth
> not to be ashamed, rightly dividing the word of truth.
> — 2 Timothy 2:15

1. Describe a mental stronghold and how it is formed.
2. List and describe two types of strongholds and give an example of each.
3. According to this lesson, what is a "high thing," and how does it exalt itself against the knowledge of God? What should be our response?

PRACTICAL APPLICATION

> But be ye doers of the word, and not hearers only,
> deceiving your own selves.
> — James 1:22

1. Have you ever dealt with a stronghold in your life? If so, what was it and how did you pull it down? Do you know someone who is currently going through something similar and would be encouraged by your testimony? Share your testimony with that person the next time you get the chance!
2. Is there an area of your life where the enemy is currently trying to build a stronghold in your mind through a lie about yourself or your situation? Find three scriptures that identify the truth concerning you or your circumstances and speak them out loud every day this week.

LESSON 20

TOPIC

Eliminating the Giants in Your Life

SCRIPTURES

1. **1 Samuel 17:1-4** — Now the Philistines gathered together their armies to battle, and were gathered together at Shochoh, which belongeth to Judah, and pitched between Shochoh and Azekah,

in Ephesdammim. And Saul and the men of Israel were gathered together, and pitched by the valley of Elah, and set the battle in array against the Philistines. And the Philistines stood on a mountain on the one side, and Israel stood on a mountain on the other side: and there was a valley between them. And there went out a champion out of the camp of the Philistines, named Goliath, of Gath, whose height was six cubits and a span.

2. **1 Samuel 17:5-7** — And he had an helmet of brass upon his head, and he was armed with a coat of mail; and the weight of the coat was five thousand shekels of brass. And he had greaves of brass upon his legs, and a target of brass between his shoulders. And the staff of his spear was like a weaver's beam; and his spear's head weighed six hundred shekels of iron: and one bearing a shield went before him.

3. **1 Samuel 17:8,9** — And he stood and cried unto the armies of Israel, and said unto them, Why are ye come out to set your battle in array? am not I a Philistine, and ye servants to Saul? choose you a man for you, and let him come down to me. If he be able to fight with me, and to kill me, then will we be your servants: but if I prevail against him, and kill him, then shall ye be our servants, and serve us.

4. **1 Samuel 17:11** — When Saul and all Israel heard those words of the Philistine, they were dismayed, and greatly afraid.

5. **1 Samuel 17:14** — And David was the youngest: and the three eldest followed Saul.

6. **1 Samuel 17:16** — And the Philistine drew near morning and evening, and presented himself forty days.

7. **1 Samuel 17:19** — Now Saul, and they, and all the men of Israel, were in the valley of Elah, fighting with the Philistines.

8. **1 Samuel 17:23-26** — And as he talked with them, behold, there came up the champion, the Philistine of Gath, Goliath by name, out of the armies of the Philistines, and spake according to the same words: and David heard them. And all the men of Israel, when they saw the man, fled from him, and were sore afraid. And the men of Israel said, Have ye seen this man that is come up? surely to defy Israel is he come up: and it shall be, that the man who killeth him, the king will enrich him with great riches, and will give him his daughter, and make his father's house free in Israel. And David spake to the men that stood by him, saying, What shall be done to the man that killeth this Philistine, and taketh away the reproach from Israel? for

who is this uncircumcised Philistine, that he should defy the armies of the living God?

9. **1 Samuel 17:28-31** — And Eliab his eldest brother heard when he spake unto the men; and Eliab's anger was kindled against David, and he said, Why camest thou down hither? and with whom hast thou left those few sheep in the wilderness? I know thy pride, and the naughtiness of thine heart; for thou art come down that thou mightest see the battle. And David said, What have I now done? Is there not a cause? And he turned from him toward another, and spake after the same manner: and the people answered him again after the former manner. And when the words were heard which David spake, they rehearsed them before Saul: and he sent for him.

10. **1 Samuel 17:32** — And David said to Saul, Let no man's heart fail because of him; thy servant will go and fight with this Philistine.

11. **1 Samuel 17:33-36** — And Saul said to David, Thou art not able to go against this Philistine to fight with him: for thou art but a youth, and he a man of war from his youth. And David said unto Saul, Thy servant kept his father's sheep, and there came a lion, and a bear, and took a lamb out of the flock: And I went out after him, and smote him, and delivered it out of his mouth: and when he arose against me, I caught him by his beard, and smote him, and slew him. Thy servant slew both the lion and the bear: and this uncircumcised Philistine shall be as one of them, seeing he hath defied the armies of the living God.

12. **1 Samuel 17:37-40** — David said moreover, The Lord that delivered me out of the paw of the lion, and out of the paw of the bear, he will deliver me out of the hand of this Philistine. And Saul said unto David, Go, and the Lord be with thee. And Saul armed David with his armour, and he put an helmet of brass upon his head; also he armed him with a coat of mail. And David girded his sword upon his armour, and he assayed to go; for he had not proved it. And David said unto Saul, I cannot go with these; for I have not proved them. And David put them off him. And he took his staff in his hand, and chose him five smooth stones out of the brook, and put them in a shepherd's bag which he had, even in a scrip; and his sling was in his hand: and he drew near to the Philistine.

13. **1 Samuel 17:41-44** — And the Philistine came on and drew near unto David; and the man that bare the shield went before him. And when the Philistine looked about, and saw David, he disdained him: for he was but a youth, and ruddy, and of a fair countenance. And the

Philistine said unto David, Am I a dog, that thou comest to me with staves? And the Philistine cursed David by his gods. And the Philistine said to David, Come to me, and I will give thy flesh unto the fowls of the air, and to the beasts of the field.

14. **1 Samuel 17:45-51** — Then said David to the Philistine, Thou comest to me with a sword, and with a spear, and with a shield: but I come to thee in the name of the Lord of hosts, the God of the armies of Israel, whom thou hast defied. This day will the Lord deliver thee into mine hand; and I will smite thee, and take thine head from thee; and I will give the carcases of the host of the Philistines this day unto the fowls of the air, and to the wild beasts of the earth; that all the earth may know that there is a God in Israel. And all this assembly shall know that the Lord saveth not with sword and spear: for the battle is the Lord's, and he will give you into our hands. And it came to pass, when the Philistine arose, and came, and drew nigh to meet David, that David hastened, and ran toward the army to meet the Philistine. And David put his hand in his bag, and took thence a stone, and slang it, and smote the Philistine in his forehead, that the stone sunk into his forehead; and he fell upon his face to the earth. So David prevailed over the Philistine with a sling and with a stone, and smote the Philistine, and slew him; but there was no sword in the hand of David. Therefore David ran, and stood upon the Philistine, and took his sword, and drew it out of the sheath thereof, and slew him, and cut off his head therewith. And when the Philistines saw their champion was dead, they fled.

15. **1 Samuel 17:54** — And David took the head of the Philistine, and brought it to Jerusalem; but he put his armour in his tent.

SYNOPSIS

The story of David facing Goliath is a perfect example and illustration of how we should deal with seemingly impossible situations. David didn't listen to the taunts and threats of the enemy. When all of Israel was terrified, David ran boldly toward Goliath in fearless faith. He rejected the natural weapons offered to him and went forward with the spiritual weapons provided by God.

The emphasis of this lesson:

Regardless of how daunting the threats of the enemy are or how impossible it may seem to overcome his attacks, when we are clothed in the full spiritual weaponry of God, we will prevail against the giants in our lives.

In this series, we have learned about the biblical meaning of warfare, what the Bible teaches about demons, the seven pieces of weaponry in the armor of God, and how to pull down strongholds and cast down imaginations. In this final lesson, we will learn from David's battle with Goliath how to eliminate the "giants" in our own life.

An Insurmountable Enemy

The story of David and Goliath begins in First Samuel 17:1-7, which says:

> **Now the Philistines gathered together their armies to battle. And Saul and the men of Israel were gathered together, and pitched by the valley of Elah, and set the battle in array against the Philistines. And the Philistines stood on a mountain on the one side, and Israel stood on a mountain on the other side: and there was a valley between them. And there went out a champion out of the camp of the Philistines, named Goliath, of Gath, whose height was six cubits and a span** [about 9 feet 9 inches tall]. **And he had an helmet of brass upon his head, and he was armed with a coat of mail; and the weight of the coat was five thousand shekels of brass. And he had greaves of brass upon his legs, and a target of brass between his shoulders. And the staff of his spear was like a weaver's beam; and his spear's head weighted six hundred shekels of iron: and one bearing a shield went before him.**

These verses describe the enemy that the armies of Irael were facing. Goliath was a giant who stood about 9 feet 9 inches tall and carried several pieces of extremely heavy armor. To give more insight into Goliath's stature and the weight of his armor, Rick read from his book, *Dressed to Kill.*

> Goliath was armed to the max! Notice that the "coat of mail" he wore weighed "five thousand shekels of brass." As I mentioned earlier, 5,000 shekels of brass is the equivalent of 125 pounds!

In addition to Goliath's helmet, and his breastplate that weighed 125 pounds, he also had greaves of brass and a target (javelin) of brass slung between his shoulders! The staff of his spear was like a weaver's beam — which means the long staff of his spear weighed at least 17 pounds. Additionally, the scripture specifically says that the spear's head weighed 600 shekels of iron — which is equivalent to 16 pounds.

One scholar has speculated that the weight of all these pieces of weaponry together — his helmet, breastplate, greaves, brass javelin, spear, and shield — may have weighed in excess of 700 pounds!

In every respect imaginable, Goliath was a frightful sight! How would you feel if you were challenged by a foe who stood 9 feet 9 inches tall and wore more than 700 pounds of weaponry? And if Goliath wore weaponry weighing that much, imagine how much the giant must have weighed himself?

Don't Listen to the Enemy

David's story continues in 1 Samuel 17:8, 9, and 11:

> **And he stood and cried unto the armies of Israel, and said unto them, Why are ye come out to set your battle in array? am not I a Philistine, and ye servants to Saul? choose you a man for you, and let him come down to me. If he be able to fight with me, and to kill me, then will we be your servants: but if I prevail against him, and kill him, then shall ye be our servants, and serve us. When Saul and all Israel heard those words of the Philistine, they were dismayed, and greatly afraid.**

If you listen to the enemy, he will try to terrorize you. Israel's first mistake was listening to the enemy. Day after day, Goliath came down into the valley to intimidate and taunt them, daring them to send out a champion for him to fight. Because of Goliath's size and the kinds of weapons he carried, the armies of Israel were dismayed and greatly afraid. They were terrified!

But then David arrived! His father had sent him to the front lines to bring food to his older brothers who were part of the army and fighting against the Philistines. First Samuel 17:14, 16, and 19 says:

And David was the youngest: and the three eldest followed Saul. And the Philistine drew near morning and evening, and presented himself forty days. Now Saul, and they, and all the men of Israel, were in the valley of Elah, fighting with the Philistines.

Goliath had been mentally bombarding and harassing the men of Israel. When David arrived, he happened to hear the threats from Goliath and asked his brothers and the other soldiers what reward there would be for the man who killed the giant.

And as he talked with them, behold, there came up the champion, the Philistine of Gath, Goliath by name, out of the armies of the Philistines, and spake according to the same words: and David heard them. And all the men of Israel, when they saw the man, fled from him, and were sore afraid. And the men of Israel said, Have ye seen this man that is come up? surely to defy Israel is he come up: and it shall be, that the man who killeth him, the king will enrich him with great riches, and will give him his daughter, and make his father's house free in Israel. And David spake to the men that stood by him, saying, What shall be done to the man that killeth this Philistine, and taketh away the reproach from Israel? for who is this uncircumcised Philistine, that he should defy the armies of the living God?
— 1 Samuel 17:23-26

Then David's brothers accused him of having impure motives and only wanting to watch the battle between Israel and the Philistines.

And Eliab his eldest brother heard when he spake unto the men; and Eliab's anger was kindled against David, and he said, Why camest thou down hither? and with whom hast thou left those few sheep in the wilderness? I know thy pride, and the naughtiness of thine heart; for thou art come down that thou mightest see the battle. And David said, What have I now done? Is there not a cause? And he turned from him toward another, and spake after the same manner: and the people answered him again after the former manner. And when the words were heard which David spake, they rehearsed them before Saul: and he sent for him.
— 1 Samuel 17:28-31

But David pointed out that Israel was just sitting back and taking the threats of the enemy. He knew there was cause to fight back against the Philistines, and he spoke up about it!

Bold Faith

All of the men of Israel were terrified of Goliath and the Philistines. Even though they were fully trained soldiers, they were so frightened that they were in a state of fear and dismay, fleeing, hiding from the enemy.

But suddenly, one young shepherd boy, David, arrived on the scene who would typically have been tending to his father's sheep. David began to speak boldly about what he was going to do with that Philistine.

In First Samuel 17:32, David said to Saul, "Let no man's heart fail because of him; thy servant will go and fight with this Philistine." First Samuel 17:33-36 records what happened next:

> **And Saul said to David, Thou art not able to go against this Philistine to fight with him: for thou art but a youth, and he a man of war from his youth. And David said unto Saul, Thy servant kept his father's sheep, and there came a lion, and a bear, and took a lamb out of the flock: And I went out after him, and smote him, and delivered it out of his mouth: and when he arose against me, I caught him by his beard, and smote him, and slew him. Thy servant slew both the lion and the bear: and this uncircumcised Philistine shall be as one of them, seeing he hath defied the armies of the living God.**
> **— 1 Samuel 17:33-36**

David was but a youth at this moment. The men of war were running away or hiding in the trenches from Goliath and the Philistine army, and along comes a young shepherd boy who says, "I'll take care of this. I'll do it. I'll take this Philistine down!"

When David went before king Saul, the king tried to discourage him. Saul was looking at David's age, his inexperience at war, and his size compared to Goliath. But David was bold and unafraid in the face of a formidable opponent. David recognized the source of his strength.

> **David said moreover, The Lord that delivered me out of the paw of the lion, and out of the paw of the bear, he will deliver me out of the hand of this Philistine. And Saul said unto David,**

Go, and the Lord be with thee. And Saul armed David with his armour, and he put an helmet of brass upon his head; also he armed him with a coat of mail. And David girded his sword upon his armour, and he assayed to go; for he had not proved it. And David said unto Saul, I cannot go with these; for I have not proved them. And David put them off him.

— 1 Samuel 17:37-39

David was just a young teenager, and Saul took all of his big, heavy armor and tried to put it on David. David was too small, and Saul's armor was too big for him to wear. The armor was very heavy, and David had never been dressed in armor before. Although Saul's armor might have protected David a little bit, because he had never worn armor, David removed it.

We can learn from David! When the enemy comes against us, we must remember that God has given us everything we will ever need to defeat the enemy. We don't need to run. We don't need to be afraid or in dismay. We have everything we need to stand against the wiles of the enemy.

Confidence in God

There are weapons of the flesh and there are weapons of the spirit. Weapons of the flesh, such as education and money, are good to have. Education is good, but education alone is not enough to deal with the enemy. Money is a good thing; it helps us in the natural. But money alone will not help us deal with the enemy. We can do everything in the natural to improve our situation, but when it comes to dealing with spiritual warfare, *we must have spiritual weapons.*

The Bible says that David refused to go against Goliath with Saul's weaponry "for he had not proved it." David was a young shepherd boy standing before the king of Israel, and even though he had an opportunity to use weapons of the flesh, he didn't want them. He had something else in mind.

And he took his staff in his hand, and chose him five smooth stones out of the brook, and put them in a shepherd's bag which he had, even in a scrip; and his sling was in his hand: and he drew near to the Philistine.

— 1 Samuel 17:40

Instead of looking toward natural weapons to defeat the enemy, David said, "I have five smooth stones from the brook in the valley of Elah." You may be wondering why David specifically chose five stones. The reason was because Goliath had four relatives who were also giants. David had no confidence in fleshly weapons, but he was very confident in the Lord and in God's spiritual weapons.

In fact, David was so confident and so precise he thought, "We have Goliath to deal with, but after I deal with him, he has four relatives who are also giants. Just in case they come after me, I'm going to bring four more stones to deal with them as well!" David was so confident in the Lord that he carried one stone to deal with each giant that he thought might come against him. That is how confident you can be when you're spiritually dressed in God's armor!

Goliath was not impressed with David's appearance. Samuel 17:41-44 says,

> **And the Philistine came on and drew near unto David; and the man that bare the shield went before him. And when the Philistine looked about, and saw David, he disdained him: for he was but a youth, and ruddy, and of a fair countenance. And the Philistine said unto David, Am I a dog, that thou comest to me with staves? And the Philistine cursed David by his gods. And the Philistine said to David, Come to me, and I will give thy flesh unto the fowls of the air, and to the beasts of the field.**

When Goliath saw David and how young he was, he mocked and cursed him. Likewise, the devil will try to mock and taunt us with his lying threats. But they are empty intimidation tactics. David's response to Goliath's threats are a great example of how believers should respond to the enemy's threats:

> **Then said David to the Philistine, Thou comest to me with a sword, and with a spear, and with a shield: but I come to thee in the name of the Lord of hosts, the God of the armies of Israel, whom thou hast defied. This day will the Lord deliver thee into mine hand; and I will smite thee, and take thine head from thee; and I will give the carcases of the host of the Philistines this day unto the fowls of the air, and to the wild beasts of the earth; that all the earth may know that there is a God in Israel. And all this assembly shall know that the Lord saveth not with sword and spear: for the battle is the Lord's, and he will give you**

into our hands. And it came to pass, when the Philistine arose, and came, and drew nigh to meet David, that David hastened, and ran toward the army to meet the Philistine. And David put his hand in his bag, and took thence a stone, and slang it, and smote the Philistine in his forehead, that the stone sunk into his forehead; and he fell upon his face to the earth. So David prevailed over the Philistine with a sling and with a stone, and smote the Philistine, and slew him; but there was no sword in the hand of David. Therefore David ran, and stood upon the Philistine, and took his sword, and drew it out of the sheath thereof, and slew him, and cut off his head therewith. And when the Philistines saw their champion was dead, they fled.

— 1 Samuel 17:45-51

David did not defeat Goliath based on his own strength. Or skill. He did not defeat the great enemy of Israel by any natural attribute or talent he possessed. David's victory over Goliath came directly from God.

First Samuel 17:54 says, "And David took the head of the Philistine, and brought it to Jerusalem; but he put his armour in his tent." David cut off the head of the giant and carried it back to Jerusalem like a trophy. He also took Goliath's weaponry as his personal trophy to remind himself that God had given him the victory over the enemy.

Friend, if you will be determined to use the weaponry God has freely given to you, you will have everything you need to put the enemy on the run! With the weapons God has given you and with the divine strategy that comes from Him, you can defeat any enemy that tries to come against you. You can act with fearless boldness, utilizing all of the weaponry God has given you to defeat every giant in your life!

STUDY QUESTIONS

Study to shew thyself approved unto God, a workman that needeth not to be ashamed, rightly dividing the word of truth.
— 2 Timothy 2:15

1. In your own words, describe why Israel was terrified at the sight of Goliath.
2. Explain why it is so important not to listen to the threats of the enemy against us.

PRACTICAL APPLICATION

But be ye doers of the word, and not hearers only,
deceiving your own selves.
—James 1:22

1. When was the last time you exercised bold faith? What was the result?

2. Think of a time when God gave you the victory over a difficult situation. What did you do to make sure you would always remember where that victory came from and who gave it to you?

3. Are you facing a troubling circumstance today? Have you been listening to the enemy or have you responded in faith? If you have been listening to the enemy, take time today to shift your mindset from fear to faith. If you have been responding in faith, take time today to thank God for giving you're the victory in this situation.

A Prayer To Receive Salvation

If you've never received Jesus as your Savior and Lord, now is the time for you to experience the new life Jesus wants to give you! To receive God's gift of salvation that can be obtained through Jesus alone, pray this prayer from your heart:

Jesus, I repent of my sin and receive You as my Savior and Lord. Wash away my sin with Your precious blood and make me completely new. I thank You that my sin is removed, and Satan no longer has any right to lay claim on me. Through Your empowering grace, I faithfully promise that I will serve You as my Lord for the rest of my life.

If you just prayed this prayer of salvation, you are born again! You are a brand-new creation in Christ! Would you please let us know of your decision by going to **renner.org/salvation**? We would love to connect with you and pray for you as you begin your new life in Christ.

Scriptures for further study: John 3:16; John 14:6; Acts 4:12; Ephesians 1:7; Hebrews 10:19,20; 1 Peter 1:18,19; Romans 10:9,10; Colossians 1:13; 2 Corinthians 5:17; Romans 6:4; 1 Peter 1:3

CLAIM YOUR FREE RESOURCE!

As a way of introducing you further to the teaching ministry of Rick Renner, we would like to send you FREE of charge his teaching, "How To Receive a Miraculous Touch From God" on CD or as an MP3 download.

In His earthly ministry, Jesus commonly healed *all* who were sick of *all* their diseases. In this profound message, learn about the manifold dimensions of Christ's wisdom, goodness, power, and love toward all humanity who came to Him in faith with their needs.

☑ **YES, I want to receive Rick Renner's monthly teaching letter!**

Simply scan the QR code to claim this resource or go to:
renner.org/claim-your-free-offer

renner.org

facebook.com/rickrenner • facebook.com/rennerdenise

youtube.com/rennerministries • youtube.com/deniserenner

instagram.com/rickrrenner • instagram.com/rennerministries_
instagram.com/rennerdenise